Strategic Training: Putting Employees First

Daniel M. Wentland

HRD Press, Inc. • Amherst • Massachusetts

Copyright © 2014, HRD Press, Inc.

Published by:

HRD Press, Inc.
22 Amherst Road
Amherst, MA 01002
800-822-2801 (U.S. and Canada)
413-253-3488
413-253-3490 (fax)
www.hrdpress.com

All rights reserved. Printed in the United States of America. No part of this material may be reproduced or utilized in any form or by any means, electronic or mechanical, including photocopying, recording, or by any information storage and retrieval system, without written permission from the publisher.

ISBN 0-87425-933-9

Production services by Jean Miller
Editorial services by Suzanne Bay
Cover design by Eileen Klockars

Table of Contents

Acknowledgments v

Preface vii

Introduction ix

Part I: Setting the Stage

Chapter 1: What is an Organization? 5

Chapter 2: Strategic Planning and
Putting Employees First 21

Chapter 3: A Deeper Journey into the Realm of
Strategy Formulation 41

Chapter 4: Scarcity 49

Part II: The Strategic Training of Employees Model (STEM)

Chapter 5: An Overview of the Strategic Training of
Employees Model (STEM) 63

Chapter 6: Task Analysis and Targeting 73

Chapter 7: Training Content (Product) 81

Chapter 8: Location Factors (Place) 95

Chapter 9: Communicating Information about Training
Programs (Promotion) 103

Chapter 10: Cost Considerations (Price) 111

Chapter 11: Implementation, Feedback, and Evaluation .. 121

Part III: Completing the Picture

Chapter 12: How the STEM Model Can Help
Organizations Solve Training Problems 131

Chapter 13: Organizational Survival 157

References 161

About the Author 169

Acknowledgments

First, I would like to express my appreciation to Bob Carkhuff and the staff at Human Resource Development Press, who gave me the opportunity to write and publish this book. I will be forever in their debt. A special word of thanks goes to Suzanne Bay, my editor, whose comments and advice made this a better book.

Along with the publishing staff, the other most important people to thank are the readers. For days, I struggled with the words to express my thanks; however, in the end, all of my attempts failed to convey how truly thankful I am to everyone who decided to read this book. I hope this will be the beginning of many writing projects we will share together.

Next, I would like to thank the following researchers and authors whose work I primarily relied upon: Stephen P. Robbins, Robert Levering, Charles Hill, Gareth Jones, Arthur Thompson Jr., A. J. Strickland III, Raymond Noe, and Michael Porter. I would also like to extend a note of appreciation to the following researchers and authors: Gregory Moorhead, Ricky Griffin, Patrick Morley, C. R. Finch, J. R. Crunkilton, Luis Gomez-Mejia, David Balkin, and Robert Cardy.

Thanks also to Glen Boyce and Michael Blankenship for their important contribution to this project. In addition, a special note of thanks goes to Dr. Joycelyn Finley-Hervey, whose inspirational teaching helped me develop the STEM model while working on my doctorate at Jackson State University in Jackson, Mississippi.

On a personal note, I would like to recognize my family—especially my wife, Kathy, who always puts up with me and makes every day seem brighter; my father, a great dad; and Shelby and Bailey, "the girls." My final thanks go to Lord Jesus Christ, from whom all blessings come.

Preface

In a recent *Wall Street Journal* article, it was reported that most organizations do not practice what they preach, despite the claims of a majority of executives that their organizations treat employees with respect and offer fair pay for the tasks performed. Nowhere is the contradiction between the words and actions of organizational leaders more apparent than training. The disconnection between what organizations say they believe and what they actually do is partly attributable to a marketing philosophy that began to dominate management theory after the production concept faded in popularity around the 1950s to 1960s. At the center of this philosophy is the notion that *the customer* should be the focus of all organizational activities and planning.

Although the emphasis upon the customer appears to be a logical premise for building organizational success, it is actually quite misleading: Simply put, many organizations do not know who their customers are! For example, who is the customer at a college or university? High school graduates? Adults returning to college? Graduate students? Individuals from other countries attending classes? Or individuals seeking a vocational trade? And what is the socio-economic and demographic data associated with these classifications of students? Who is the customer for a retailer like Wal Mart? Is it the person who drives a Mercedes to Wal Mart in order to purchase everyday items at lower prices? Or is it the individual who uses public transportation to arrive at the store? A customer who cannot be specifically identified in every detail is an illusion, and illusions serve as a poor basis for building successful strategy.

And once the "customer" has been identified, should he or she be placed at the center of every organizational activity? Doing so, I believe, pushes aside the true essence of the organization, minimizing its significance. **The heart of an organization is its employees and its members.** The abilities, decisions, plans, training, and actions of the employees of an organization are what draw individuals to a particular college or retailer or even to purchase a product or pay for a service. The primary driving force that brings people into a concert hall is to hear enchanting music performed by trained musicians whose skills and talents are on display. Highly qualified employees produce quality products and provide quality service that satisfies consumer needs.

Strategic Training: Putting Employees First

An organization's employees have always made the difference between a truly successful organization and a mediocre entity, but it's amazing how often managers overlook or discount this fundamental recipe for economic survival. Organizations with cultures that focus on their people and that invest in their future will, in the long run, be more competitive than cultures that view employees as mere costs to be reduced in times of trouble.

My premise here is that an organization that plans every action around its employees will thrive in the marketplace. The Wegmans chain of grocery stores headquartered in Rochester, New York, has repeatedly been cited as one of the best employers in the United States to work for. The company's focus on its employees has made Wegmans a shining example of a local, family-managed organization that effectively and efficiently competes against national and international grocery chains.

Putting employees first and providing a quality training environment are the underlying themes of this book.

Introduction
The Link between Organizational Success and Employee Training

In the early 1980s, U.S. Steel (now USX) underwent massive downsizing and invested more than $1 billion to upgrade and computerize its production processes. To make the new technology pay off, it had to upgrade worker skills. However, during the restructuring process, the company eliminated an apprenticeship program that provided in-depth training and a number of production areas. Now it needed a training program that would cut across those specialized craft lines. USX learned that investments in physical resources often require investments in human resources (Gomez-Majia et al. 1995).

Employee training should not be a side issue that is only considered after every other detail has been carefully planned and accounted for. It must be made an integral part of any planning process, because the success or failure of every organizational activity is ultimately determined by the abilities of the employees. Organizational achievements flow from the productivity generated by the employees, which is directly related to the training provided to the employees: It's this training, after all, that prepares the employees to accomplish the tasks they are expected to perform.

Organizational survival depends on organizational training, just as the soft, beautiful petals of a precious flower rely on the plant's stems and roots to gather life-sustaining nutrients from the environment. To brush off the importance of employee training is to make a dangerous and strategic mistake. Can you imagine a professional sports team failing to establish an extensive training program that will systematically develop its athletes? Or a military unit failing to provide adequate training to improve each soldier's knowledge and abilities?

So why do some organizations seem to minimize employee training and development? The reality is that to be competitive in today's global economy, many organizations devote substantial financial resources to employee training and development, yet they fail to elevate the training function to a leading role in the organization. One pivotal challenge confronting organizational leaders is to establish quality employee training programs that will maximize the dollars spent on employee training, while at the same time increase organizational competitiveness. The information in this book provides a practical solution.

A Final Comment

An organization that invests in its employees achieves success in the marketplace. This investment in human capital must begin with the hiring process and continue throughout the employee's tenure with the company. A continual investment in human capital means providing a comprehensive and equitable employment package that, at the minimum, consists of a reasonable pay scale, benefits, and training. In this book, the first in a series that will stress the importance of putting employees first, the emphasis will be on training and the vital role that it plays in increasing the value of an organization's products and services.

Former U.S. Secretary of Labor Robert Reich strongly believes that when businesses put money into improving the skills of their workers, the investments pay off in increased productivity and improved quality of life for the workers. In his 2002 book *I'll Be Short,* he cited these examples: Granite Rock, a construction materials supplier in Watsonville, California, invests more than $2,000 per employee annually in training—nearly thirteen times the industry average. Workers at Cin-Made, an Ohio firm that makes specialized packaging, receive extensive on-the-job training and additional pay for acquiring advanced skills. And Harley-Davidson, maker of the legendary motorcycles, has established an on-site learning center for its employees.

Part I:
Setting the Stage

When a group of individuals become a "we," a harmonious whole, then the highest is reached that humans as creatures can reach.

— Albert Einstein

Chapter 1
What Is an Organization?

Have you ever worked for an organization where it felt like no one cared about you and that your contribution to the organization was always minimized? Unfortunately, I have worked for several organizations like that, with the worse being a situation where senior officials thought they were the greatest things on earth and the rest of us were there to do their bidding. The message emanating throughout that institution consisted of fear and intimidation. Each employee dreaded every work day, and very few employees went beyond what was required to do their jobs. Just trying to make it to Friday was the fuel that kept you going.

Gaining an insight into the dynamics within an organization is an endeavor that has its roots embedded in systems theory. A *system* is a group of interrelated or interacting elements forming a unified whole that works toward a common goal by accepting inputs and producing outputs in an organized transformation process. A dynamic system essentially has three basic interacting components or functions: an input function that involves capturing and assembling elements that enter the system to be processed; a processing element or transformation process that converts an input into an output; and the output that has been produced. A cybernetic system includes two additional components: feedback and control. *Feedback* is the data about the performance of a system. *Control* involves monitoring and evaluating feedback to determine whether or not a system is moving toward the achievement of its goal(s). In addition, a system can either be classified as an open system or an adaptive system. An *open system* is a system that interacts with other systems in its environment. An *adaptive system* has the ability to change itself or its environment in order to survive.

Every organization has all three components: input, processing, and output. An effective and efficient organization has all five system components working together as a harmonious whole—these three, as well as feedback and control. Thus, systems theory provides a meaningful methodology for examining the workings of an organization as it interacts with other organizations throughout the global business environment.

Another framework for conceptualizing what constitutes a system is provided by Patrick Morley in his book *Coming Back to God*. "The 'collection' of ideas we embrace forms a system that guides our choices, and hence shapes the course of our future. Here's the problem: If the 'system' you build will not work, you will not know it doesn't work for ten or twenty years. By then, damage is done and you will have given the best years of your life to a system that has failed you" (Morley 2001).

Morley's main point is that the system that has been established was designed to produce the results or outcomes that are occurring, whether those outcomes are positive or negative. From an organizational perspective, what can be learned from Morley's ideas? The ramifications are quite clear: If your organization is under-performing, it is the systems that have been established within the organization that are producing those poor results. To correct the situation, those systems must be either modified or abandoned (in which case new systems will need to be developed).

Morley's explanation of a system has been captured in the management literature by the term "organizational culture." In his book *Organizational Behavior,* Stephen P. Robbins alluded to the impact of the culture of an organization when he described how Mitsubishi Motors lost $846 million during a single fiscal year in the late 1990s. The company's strategy of relying on weak truck and bus markets in Asia and its inability to quickly respond to the demand for minivans and sport utility vehicles contributed to its financial loss.

"The real culprit, however, is the deeply rooted Mitsubishi culture: Its tradition-based culture is better suited to the automobile industry that existed in the 1970s than the one that exists today," Robbins writes. The culture of an organization influences how every task is performed, because it sets the workplace parameters that determine the overall ability of an organization to formulate and achieve its strategic objectives. Organizational culture is a primary factor that explains why one organization succeeds while another entity fails, even though both organizations are producing quality products at competitive prices.

The realization that organizational culture can positively or negatively impact organizational performance is nothing new; in fact, it can be traced back to the concept of institutionalization, whereby an organization takes on a life of its own well beyond the original vision of the founder(s). The management literature contains many descriptive characterizations of organizational culture that illustrate the positive and negative aspects of an organization's culture. However, what is missing in most of the research is a discussion of the relationship to overall financial competitiveness, based on the organization's specific culture. As stated by Eric Singleton, the director of global e-business at Raytheon Company in Lexington, Massachusetts, "If you can't describe something in business numerically, you're not doing your job properly."

To move beyond descriptive characterizations of organizational culture, we will identify three workplace parameters that form the boundaries for four specific organizational cultures. These four organizational cultures, in turn, set the stage for the development of our Financial Status Model of Organizational Culture (FSMOC). This model can be used to classify and, more importantly, predict the financial status of an organization based on its culture, with the ultimate objective of developing a course of action that will improve the organization's culture and thus its financial situation. The FSMOC model is a flexible analytical tool that can be used in any organizational setting (mechanistic, organic, profit, nonprofit, and so forth). It opens the door to a new perspective of research regarding the quantification of organizational culture by offering a framework for predicting the financial competitiveness of an organization based on the *culture* of the organization. The development of the FSMOC model provides a unique vision for estimating the financial competitiveness of an organization.

Once we explain the model, we will devote the remainder of the chapter to highlighting the connection between organizational culture (the "people factor" within an organization) and employee training as a decisive tool for modeling the level of success an organization can achieve. Ultimately, it's the quality of the people within an organization that will determine the fate of an organization. It is the training provided to the members of an organization that determines the quality of the people. Employee training and organizational success are tightly linked.

At this point, let us provide a better explanation of organizational structure, design, and culture.

Organizational Structure and Design

In 1832, Charles Babbage suggested that the scientific method with an emphasis on planning and the division of labor offered an effective framework to organize the activities conducted within an organization. In the work of sociologist Max Weber, a more comprehensive description of a bureaucracy emerged: an organization that is characterized by division of labor, managerial oversight, and the establishment of rules and regulations to govern behavior. Since then, the definitions have continued to flow as each researcher attempted to craft their vision of what is an organization.

Broadly, the term *organization* refers to a group of people working together to attain common goals. Utilizing a systems theory approach, Juecher and Fisher (1998) described an organization as a system with three distinct subsystems: First, the *why:* why the organization exists and where it's going. Next comes the *what:* what the organization does to pursue its purpose and accomplish its mission. The third subsystem is the *how:* how the individuals, teams, divisions, departments, and other subgroups interact. Still other researchers have described organizations by their structure: how job tasks are formally divided, grouped, and coordinated. These researchers utilize terms such as *work specialization, departmentalization, the chain of command, the span of control, centralization* versus *decentralization,* and *formalization.*

Another research approach focuses on the design of the organization. The most common organizational designs are the simple structure, the bureaucracy, the matrix structure, the team structure, the virtual organization, and the boundless organization. From the concepts of organizational structure and design, the notion of a mechanistic or organic organization has evolved in the management literature. The *mechanistic* model is a structure characterized by extensive departmentalization, high formalization, a limited information network, and centralization. The *organic* model is a structure that is flat, uses cross-hierarchical and cross-functional teams, has low formalization, possesses a comprehensive information network, and relies on participative decision making.

A recent quantitative approach to characterizing the structure of an organization was presented in a paper by Ronda F. Reigle (2001). In this paper, Reigle developed the organizational culture assessment (OCA) tool, which provided a mechanism for quantifying whether an organization was mechanistic, mechanistic-organic, organic-mechanistic, or organic.

From the body of research devoted to studying organizational development, three common elements have been cited to describe an organization: (1) people, (2) a goal or purpose, and (3) a structure (meaning any phenomena created by the members of an organization) that defines and limits the behavior of members of an organization. Put simply, without people, a goal or purpose, and some form of structure, there is no organization! Of the three elements of an organization, *people* constitute the most important factor, because without human beings, the other two elements cease to exist.

Once the three elements of an organization are brought together and an organization is formed, a culture develops. That culture should concern every organizational decision maker. For our purposes, the term *organizational decision makers* can include any member of an organization, from the CEO to the shop foreman (and non-administrative personnel, if those individuals or groups are empowered to make organizational decisions). The term *group* can apply to any combination of two or more individuals who have the authority to make organizational decisions. Organizational decisions can range from day-to-day workflow procedures to strategic planning objectives.

What is Organizational Culture?

Organizational culture is "the way we do things around here." Two of the most comprehensive definitions of organizational culture are listed below.

> "The pattern of basic assumptions that a given group has invented, discovered, or developed in learning to cope with its problems of external adaptation and internal integration" (Schein 1985).

> "A set of symbols, ceremonies, and myths that communicate the underlying values and beliefs of that organization to its employees" (Ouchi 1981).

Moving beyond the definitional claims of organizational culture, we can use three workplace parameters to help us create a framework for measuring four distinct organizational cultures. However, before we explore these parameters, let's examine some research regarding the financial impact of organizational culture.

Organizational culture is important because organizational culture influences the bottom line. Any individual who has held an administrative position knows that financial results are closely monitored. It does not matter if an organization is described as profit, nonprofit, mechanistic, organic, or a matrix structure—the bottom line is the bottom line. For our purposes, the definition of "the bottom line" will be a broad one: any financial measurement relating to an organization (e.g., profit or loss, return on total assets, stock price, revenue or market share growth, or return on equity). So what is the bottom line regarding the impact of organizational culture?

In a research paper titled "Five Conditions for High-Performance Cultures," the authors Juechter and Fisher cited the work of John P. Kotter, James L. Heskett, and Daniel Denison. Kotter and Heskett demonstrated in their book *Corporate Culture and Performance* that the culture of an organization has a significant effect on a firm's long-term sustainability and economic performance. A 15-year study by Daniel Denison concluded that culture affects an organization's ability to support sustainable success. Denison's research was done on more than 1,000 companies of different sizes, sectors, industries, and ages. Other studies (Barney, 1986; Kopelman, Brief, and Guzzo, 1990; Thompson and Luthans, 1990; Weick, 1985; Wilkins and Ouchi, 1983) indicate that the culture of an organization has positive economic consequences.

Organizational decision makers still need tools that can quantify the culture of their organization, predict the financial status of their organization based on its culture, and provide guidance in terms of how to improve the financial status of the organization. The linkage between the culture of an organization, its financial status, and the proposing of a course of action to improve the financial status of an organization is contained in the Financial Status Model of Organizational Culture (FSMOC).

To move forward with the development of the FSMOC model, let's return to our examination of the three workplace parameters that go beyond descriptive characterizations of organizational culture. These workplace parameters of organizational culture can be applied to the organization as a whole or to any sub-unit within an organization.

Workplace Parameters

Throughout the literature, these three workplace parameters emerge as a common, overriding framework for understanding organizational culture: (1) managerial attitudes and practices in the workplace, (2) the organizational environment among the employees, and (3) the tasks being performed within the organization.

Managerial Attitudes and Practices in the Workplace. Managerial attitudes and practices in the workplace can be assessed by the overall degree of trust or lack of trust between administrative and non-administrative personnel. An adversarial relationship between administrative and non-administrative personnel tends to develop when management focuses too much on operational, financial, and marketing issues while ignoring or paying limited attention to the well-being of its employees. Dissatisfied employees purposely engage in many behaviors that limit productivity and compromise organizational success. A fertile breeding ground for advancing productivity and promoting organizational success can only be laid when individuals are respected for who they are and placed in positions that complement their strengths. And make no mistake about it: Increasing productivity is the driving force behind economic survival. William J. Baumol and Alan S. Blinder in their 2000 book *Economics: Principles and Policies* put it this way:

> Only rising productivity can raise standards of living in the long run. Over long periods of time, small differences in rates of productivity growth compound like interest in a bank account and can make an enormous difference to a society's prosperity. Nothing contributes more to material well-being, to the reduction of poverty, to increases in leisure time, and to a country's ability to finance education, public health, environmental improvement, and the arts than its productivity growth rate.

From a strict organizational perspective, the right managerial attitude can breathe life into a management philosophy or culture that will boost the chances of organizational success by establishing a workplace environment in which individuals will want to consistently perform at their best. "A social organization premised on equity, security, and participation will generate greater productivity than one premised on greed and fear," Reich wrote in 1983. Robert Levering had this to say about organizations where there is trust between administrative and non-administrative personnel: "The dynamic of relentless self-interest is supplanted by a different kind of relationship, where both sides find common ground to work together for their mutual benefit without compromising their separate interests" (Levering 1988).

The Organizational Environment Among the Employees. The organizational environment among the employees can be assessed by the extent of cooperation and internal politics and favoritism within the organization. A highly politicized work environment will eat away at collegiality and undermine productivity. If left unchecked, it will eventually squelch innovation, cripple productivity, and destroy the organization. The long-term survival of any organization will depend on whether or not it controls internal politics and favoritism. Any organization that fails to base performance and compensation on merit will drift into mediocrity and possibly face extinction in the global marketplace. Merit must be rewarded; favoritism must be discouraged.

The Tasks Being Performed within an Organization. The tasks being performed within an organization can be assessed by asking whether or not a task has meaning for that individual. A recent study of 50,000 employees at 60 organizations found that most employees don't understand how their work contributes to the organization's goals and vision. Individuals tend to be more productive when they sense that their work means something and that they "mean something," and when they feel that their organization is making a positive impact on society. The recent financial scandals regarding Enron, WorldCom, Qwest, HealthSouth, and so forth illustrate the negative impact of an organizational culture that fosters unethical behavior.[*]

A culture of what Alan Greenspan, former chairman of the Federal Reserve, calls "infectious greed" eventually cripples an organization. On the other hand, organizations that create an environment where individuals feel that their work is important and that their organization is providing a positive benefit to the community set the stage for innovation and creativity. When innovation and creativity flourish, so will productivity—the driving force behind economic growth and survival.

Using the three workplace parameters as our base, we lay the foundation to identify four distinct organizational cultures.

---

[*] As noted in 2003 by legal scholar Marianne M. Jennings, any organization involved in regulatory or criminal violations or product-liability litigation tends to experience a long-term deterioration in financial performance.

Measuring Organizational Culture

How do we measure culture? Using the three critical workplace parameters of attitude, environment, and tasks, we can establish criteria for measuring the culture of an organization. Then we can assess the financial status of that organization.

Managerial Attitudes and Practices in the Workplace

Individuals tend to trust the administration when operational, financial, marketing, and employee satisfaction issues are given equal attention by management.

Individuals tend to distrust the administration when management focuses on operational, financial, and marketing issues, yet ignores employee satisfaction issues or gives them only limited attention.

The Organizational Environment

The ideal environment is one in which cooperation among individuals and departments/units is encouraged, politicking and favoritism are discouraged, and performance and compensation issues are based on merit.

An atmosphere of non-cooperation exists when cooperation among individuals and departments/units is discouraged, politicking and favoritism are encouraged, and performance and compensation issues are not based on merit.

The Tasks Being Performed Within an Organization

The task has meaning to the individual when he or she feels that his or her actions have a meaningful impact on the organization. The individual should feel that the organization stands for something more than just the pursuit of profits—that it also contributes to the welfare of the community. In addition, the organization must pursue ethical behavior in accomplishing its daily and long-term strategic objectives.

Tasks do not have meaning if individuals feel that their actions have no meaningful impact on the organization, the organization does not stand for something more than just the pursuit of profits, and the organization encourages a culture of infectious greed.

With our measurement criteria established, we can now see four distinct organizational cultures:

Organizational Culture A:
- There is a relationship of trust between administrative and non-administrative personnel.
- Cooperation between individuals and departments/units is encouraged and politicking and favoritism are discouraged.
- Individuals feel that their actions have a meaningful impact on the organization.

Organizational Culture B:
- Two of the three elements of organizational culture "A" are present (e.g., trust and cooperation). However, the tasks might not have meaning for the individual.

Organizational Culture D:
- One of the three elements of organizational culture "A" are present (e.g., the tasks might have meaning for the individual, but there is no trust or cooperation present within the culture of the organization).

Organizational Culture F:
- None of the three elements of organizational culture "A" are present.

Now that we have identified four measurable and distinct organizational cultures, we can present the FSMOC model.

What Is an Organization?

The Financial Status Model of Organizational Culture (FSMOC)

Organizational Culture A

Measurement Criteria	Financial Status of Organization	Recommended Course of Action
1. Trust 2. Cooperation 3. Task has meaning	Higher financial performance, compared to other organizations within the same industry	Continue present policies and practices

Organizational Culture B

Two of the three "A" elements of organizational culture are present	Competitive financial performance, compared to other organizations within the same industry	Incorporate the missing element of organizational culture "A" into the "B" culture

Organizational Culture D

One of the three "A" elements of organizational culture is present	Below-average financial performance, compared to other organizations within the same industry	Incorporate the two missing elements of organizational culture "A" into the "D" culture

Organizational Culture F

1. Distrust 2. Non-cooperation 3. Task does not have meaning	Significantly below-average financial performance, compared to other organizations within the same industry	Incorporate the three missing elements of organizational culture "A" into the "F" culture

According to the FSMOC model, organizations that have a type "A" culture are predicted to out-perform their competition. Financial measurements that can be used to test this assumption include earnings per share, sales volume, return on equity, stock price, operational costs, and net profit. As for policy recommendations, the FSMOC model suggests that administrative personnel should continue with their current practices.

Organizations that have a type "B" culture are predicted to be financially competitive with other organizations within the same industry. The policy recommendation for these organizations is to incorporate within their organizational culture the missing organizational culture "A" element, and thus form a type "A" culture.

Organizations that have a type "D" culture are predicted to perform below their competitors. The policy recommendation for these organizations is to develop a type "B" or "A" organizational culture.

Organizations that have a type "F" culture are predicted to perform significantly below their competitors. The policy recommendation for these organizations is to incorporate the missing elements of organizational cultures "D," "B," and "A."

The FSMOC Model and the Bottom Line

Our financial status model, FSMOC, links the culture of an organization and the financial status of that organization. In addition, the model provides decision makers with a methodology to improve the financial status of their organization by adopting an administrative philosophy that fosters a type "A" or "B" organizational culture. It elevates the analysis regarding organizational culture by quantifying the culture of an organization in order to predict its financial performance, while also providing a course of action to improve the organization's culture and thus its bottom line. In the final analysis, this is what business is all about!

The FSMOC Model, the "People Factor," and Employee Training

Organizational cultures A, B, D, and F provide a framework for understanding organizational performance—a framework built on three critical workplace parameters: managerial attitudes and practices in the workplace; the organizational environment among the employees; and the tasks being performed within an organization.

At the core of the FSMOC lies a common thread that binds each of the three critical workplace parameters together. This common thread is the driving force that ultimately determines whether or not an organization will possess an A, B, D, or F organizational culture, so it has a fundamental influence on the level of success an organization can achieve. So what is this common thread? The "people" element is the most important factor in any organization. The quality and attitudes of the people within an organization set the stage for its accomplishments. Thus, to understand organizational performance, one must understand the "people factor" within an organization. What influences the quality of the people within an organization? The training provided to those individuals.

In sum, the quality of an organization's people, at all levels, determines organizational success or failure because an organization is nothing more than the system(s) that the members of the organization created, and the superiority of any creation ultimately depends on the abilities of its creator(s). Thus, at the core of organizational performance is the quality of the members of an organization. Failing to recognize this truism leaves the organization in peril.

The remainder of this book is organized to lead you step-by-step toward a comprehensive understanding of the Strategic Training of Employees Model (STEM) that was introduced in the Winter 2003 volume of *Advanced Management Journal.* The STEM model provides a new insight for increasing the value of the product and/or service that organizations bring to the marketplace by providing corporate leaders with a practical methodology for enhancing their organization's investment in its most important asset—its people.

The STEM model consists of a macro-organizational training level analysis, a micro-organizational training level analysis, and an implementation, feedback, and evaluation section. The macro-organizational training level focuses on linking the strategic planning goals of an organization with its training objectives. The micro-organizational training level analysis focuses on developing specific training programs. A task analysis links the macro and micro organizational training levels together. Finally, the implementation, feedback, and evaluation portion of the STEM model provides information regarding the quality of the training.

A fundamental premise of the STEM model is to link organizational training with the strategic objectives of an organization. We will examine the strategic planning process in the next chapter.

Strategic Training: Putting Employees First

Critical Points in Chapter 1

Critical Point 1

Three critical workplace parameters are (1) managerial attitudes and practices in the workplace, (2) the organizational environment, and (3) the tasks being performed within an organization.

Critical Point 2

These workplace parameters form the foundation of the Financial Status Model of Organizational Culture (FSMOC).

Critical Point 3

The Financial Status model establishes a framework to evaluate the culture of an organization, and provides a methodology for improving the culture and financial performance of an organization.

Critical Point 4

At the core of the three workplace parameters and the Financial Status model is the quality of the employees and members of an organization.

Critical Point 5

One primary factor impacting the quality of the members of an organization is the training that those members receive. Failing to recognize this fact puts the organization in serious jeopardy.

> For want of a nail, the horse was lost; for want of a horse, the rider was lost; for want of a rider, the battle was lost; for want of a battle, the kingdom was lost; and all for the want of a horseshoe nail.
>
> – Anonymous

Chapter 2
Strategic Planning and Putting Employees First

Taking care of first things first—understanding why an organization exists, and examining how it can continue to survive against competing entities—brings us into the realm of strategic planning.

The business landscape is littered with examples of companies that have failed to maximize stakeholder value because they lost their direction or drifted into all sorts of business ventures without first acquiring the knowledge and expertise to manage those ventures. A classic example is Sears, which in 1981 expanded into real estate and financial services, only to experience a decline in its core business of retailing. By 1993, Sears had sold all its financial units, yet it continued to experience sales and image problems in its retailing division. Sears has still not recovered from its management team's misadventure into uncharted waters (where Sears had limited or no experience). The company's series of missteps culminated when Kmart took over Sears in November of 2004. The once-powerful number-one retailer in the nation was reduced to the status of take-over victim, and is now playing a secondary role to another struggling retail company. The lesson to be learned is that poor managerial decisions can cause a company to lose its identity, resulting in an overall lack of direction and purpose that eventually diverts and dilutes the human resource capabilities of an organization. Sears was a major retailer, but when it lost its focus on retail, its financial performance eroded.

The role of strategic planning is to keep an organization on track and focused on the activities that it does best so that it does not drift into mediocrity. Strategic planning should improve management decision making and give the company a competitive advantage or allow it to remain competitive in the marketplace. The hallmarks of strategic planning are analysis, development of a course of action aimed at achieving a competitive advantage, implementation of that course of action, constant feedback, and taking corrective measures when necessary. The holy grail of the strategic planning process is to learn how to make better managerial decisions, as measured by the competitive advantage that the organization achieves over its rivals.

```
┌──────────────┐     ┌──────────────┐     ┌──────────────────┐
│  Engage in   │     │   Improve    │     │  Establish a     │
│  Strategic   │ ──▶ │  managerial  │ ──▶ │  competitive     │
│  Planning    │     │  decision    │     │  advantage       │
│              │     │  making      │     │  for the         │
│              │     │              │     │  organization    │
│              │     │              │     │  in the          │
│              │     │              │     │  marketplace     │
└──────────────┘     └──────────────┘     └──────────────────┘
```

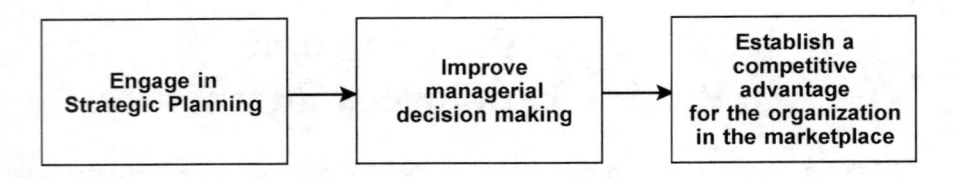

Managerial Decision Making

Systems engineering pioneer Andrew Sage defines managerial decision making as *the processes of thought and action involving an irrevocable allocation of resources that culminates in choice behavior.* "The quality of a decision depends on how well the decision maker is able to acquire information, to analyze information, and to evaluate and interpret information such as to discriminate between relevant and irrelevant bits of data," Sage wrote in 1981. Henry Mintzberg identified four basic roles that managerial decision makers tend to assume in an organization: the *entrepreneur*, who voluntarily initiates change; the *disturbance handler*, who assists in settling disputes; the *resource allocator*, who decides how scarce organizational resources will be distributed; and finally a *negotiator*, who represents the organization in reaching agreements with other organizations. The quality of the decision is influenced by skills that the manager possesses. Most successful managers have a battery of technical, interpersonal, conceptual, and diagnostic skills that they use quite effectively.

Technical skills: Skills necessary to accomplish specific tasks within the organization

Interpersonal skills: Skills that make up the manager's ability to communicate with, understand, and motivate individuals and groups

Conceptual skills: Skills that have to do with thinking in the abstract

Diagnostic skills: Skills that involve understanding cause-and-effect relationships and recognizing the optimal solutions to a problem

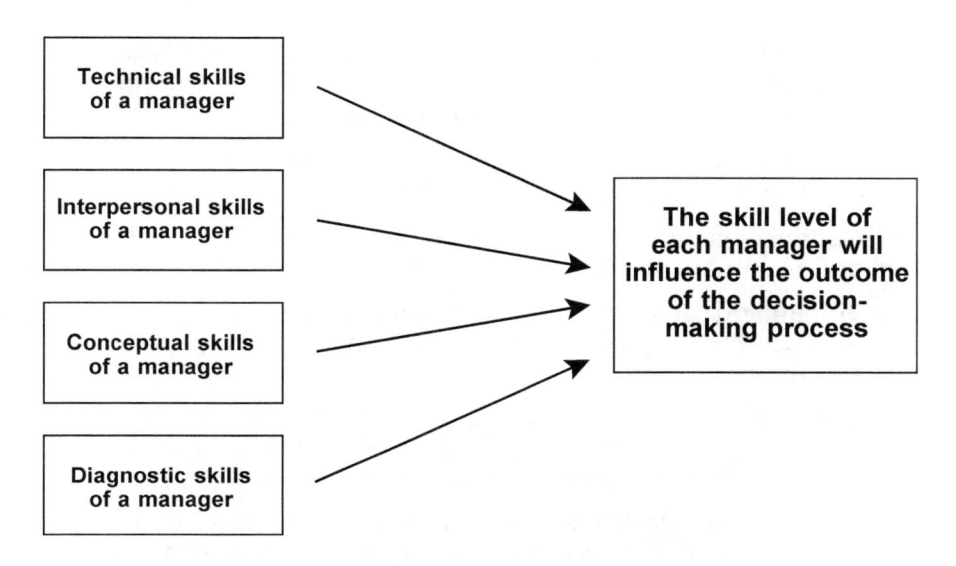

```
┌──────────────────┐
│ Technical skills │──────────↘
│   of a manager   │            ↘
└──────────────────┘              ↘
┌──────────────────┐                ┌────────────────────┐
│Interpersonal skills│──────────→   │  The skill level of │
│   of a manager   │              →│  each manager will │
└──────────────────┘              →│ influence the outcome│
┌──────────────────┐              →│   of the decision-  │
│ Conceptual skills│──────────→    │   making process    │
│   of a manager   │                └────────────────────┘
└──────────────────┘              ↗
┌──────────────────┐            ↗
│ Diagnostic skills│──────────↗
│   of a manager   │
└──────────────────┘
```

Decision-making Models

Numerous models have been established to illustrate the decision-making process, including the optimizing decision-making model, the so-called "satisficing" model, the implicit favorite model, organizational procedures view, intuitive model, political view, and individual differences perspective.

Optimizing Decision-making Model. This first decision-making model can be traced back to the "rational manager" view. This is the classic conception of decision making in organizations, developed from the microeconomic notion of a rational, completely informed, single decision maker. In this model of decision making, the decision maker proceeds through six steps that result in the selection of the optimal solution:

1. Ascertain the need for a decision.
2. Identify the decision criteria.
3. Allocate weights to the criteria.
4. Develop the alternatives.
5. Evaluate the alternatives.
6. Select the best alternative.

Lurking behind these steps is the assumption of rationality—the notion that choices are consistent and value maximizing. The decision maker displays several characteristics:

Goal-orientation: The decision maker has a single, well-defined goal that he or she is trying to maximize.

Options: The decision maker is fully comprehensive in his or her ability to assess criteria and alternatives.

Preferences: Rationality assumes that the criteria and alternatives can be assigned numerical values and ranked in a preferential order.

Constancy: The same criteria and alternatives should be obtained every time; the specific decision criteria are constant; and the weights assigned to them are stable over time.

Outcome: The final choice will maximize the outcome because the decision maker will select the alternative that rates the highest.

Satisficing Model. The second decision-making model uses the satisficing model and world-renowned economist Herbert Simon's concept of bounded rationality. (Simon coined the term *satisfice*. It is presumed to relate to both *satisfy* and *suffice*.) The general premise of bounded rationality is this, as first explained by Simon: Individuals make decisions by constructing simplified models that extract the essential features from problems without capturing all their complexity (Robbins 1993). A decision maker selects the first solution that is good enough to solve the issue at hand. In other words, satisficing refers to decision making that seeks an acceptable solution, as opposed to an optimal solution.

Implicit Favorite Model. A third managerial decision-making model is the implicit favorite model. In this decision-making model, the decision maker selects an alternative early in the decision process, and tends to be less objective about all the other choices.

Organizational Procedures View. A fourth model referred to as the organizational procedures view stems from the work of R. M. Cyert and J. G. March's *A Behavioral Theory of the Firm,* published in 1963. In this theory, the desire to identify organizational roles, channels of communication, and relationships drives decision making. The formal and informal structure of an organization, its standard operating procedures, and its channels of communication are the important variables influencing decision making.

Intuitive Model. A fifth managerial decision-making model is called the intuitive model. In this model, the decision maker makes a decision based on his or her experience. In this case, the decision-making process and rational analysis work together.

Political View. According to a sixth model of decision making (the political view), all decisions are determined as an outcome of power and influence. Power, influence, compromising, and negotiation are among various organizational factors and units that influence a decision.

Individual Differences Perspective. A final model of managerial decision making is the individual differences perspective. In this model, the problem-solving and information-processing capabilities of a decision maker are the most important factors influencing the decision-making process. Important in this theory is the concept of cognitive complexity and the "U-curve." The U-curve hypothesis from H. M. Schroder, M. J. Driver, and S. Steufert (1967) implies that a decision maker can only process a certain amount of information, given a certain environmental complexity (up to a maximum point), after which the information processing of a decision maker is diminished.

The strategic planning process provides a framework for focusing a decision maker's attention on creating a competitive advantage.

Decision-Making Models
The Optimizing Decision Model
The Satisficing Model
The Implicit Favorite Model
Organizational Procedures View
The Intuitive Model
The Political View Model
The Individual Differences Perspective

→ A decision maker can only process a limited amount of information. → The strategic planning process provides a framework for focusing a decision maker's attention on creating a competitive advantage.

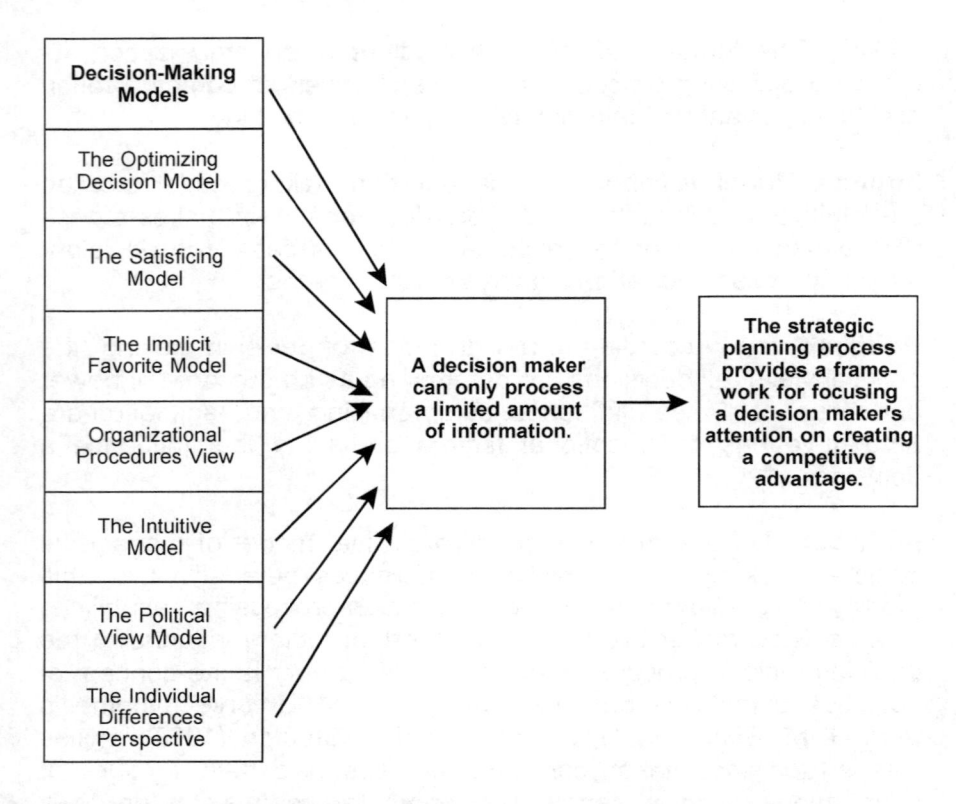

The Strategic Planning Process

In 1980, Derek F. Abell proposed that the framework of the strategic planning process could be built on the answers to three critical questions:

- Who is being satisfied?
- What is being satisfied?
- How are the needs of the customers being satisfied?

If you determine who is being satisfied, you can identify the customer base (or target market). The other two questions focus attention on the needs of the target market, and how an organization can best meet those needs. In essence, the three questions proposed by Abell form the basis by which organizational decision makers identify or define the purpose of the organization.

```
┌─────────────────┐
│   Who is being  │──────────┐
│    satisfied?   │           ╲
└─────────────────┘            ╲
                                ▶
┌─────────────────┐       ┌──────────────────────┐
│  What is being  │──────▶│ Define the purpose of│
│   satisfied?    │       │   an organization.   │
└─────────────────┘       └──────────────────────┘
                                ▲
┌─────────────────┐            ╱
│ How are the needs│           ╱
│ of the customers │──────────┘
│ being satisfied? │
└─────────────────┘
```

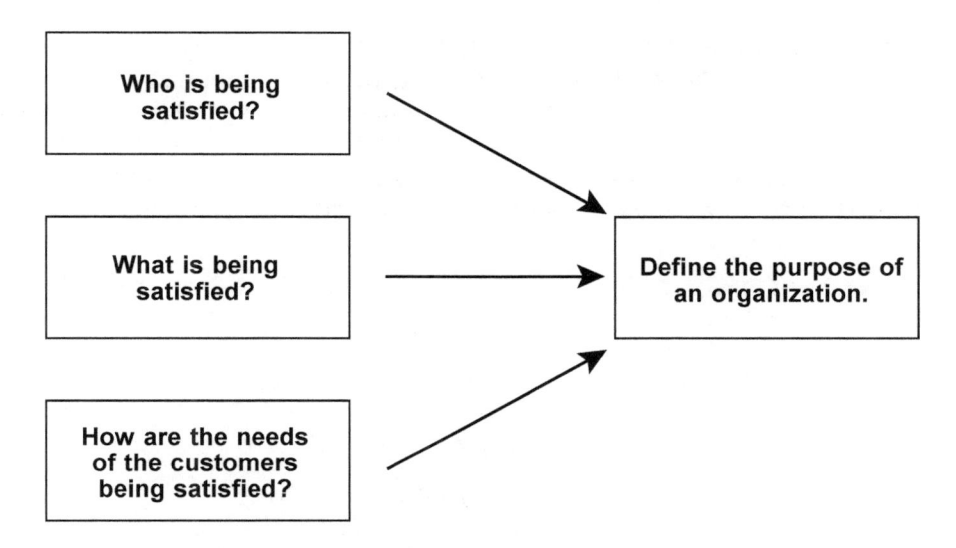

Thus, the strategic planning process is utilized to systematically address the questions proposed by Abell; it is also the phase during which managers choose a set of strategies. The strategic planning process consists of five basic steps that can be followed simultaneously.

Step 1. Formulate the corporate mission and vision statements, and identify the major organizational goals.

Step 2. Analyze the organization's external competitive environment to identify opportunities and threats.

Step 3. Analyze the organization's internal operating environment to identify the organization's strengths and weaknesses.

Step 4. Select strategies that build on the organization's strengths and correct its weaknesses, to take advantage of external opportunities and counter external threats.

Step 5. Implement strategy. Design appropriate organizational structures and control systems to put the organization's chosen strategy into action.

If we look at strategic planning from a different angle, we see that the process can be separated into two dimensions: strategy and operational effectiveness. Michael Porter, a business professor at Harvard University (and probably the leading authority on strategic planning) believes that *strategy* is a plan for competing in the marketplace, whereas *operational effectiveness* is the ability to perform operational tasks more efficiently than do competitors. The end product of the strategic planning process for an organization should be to establish a competitive advantage over its rivals.

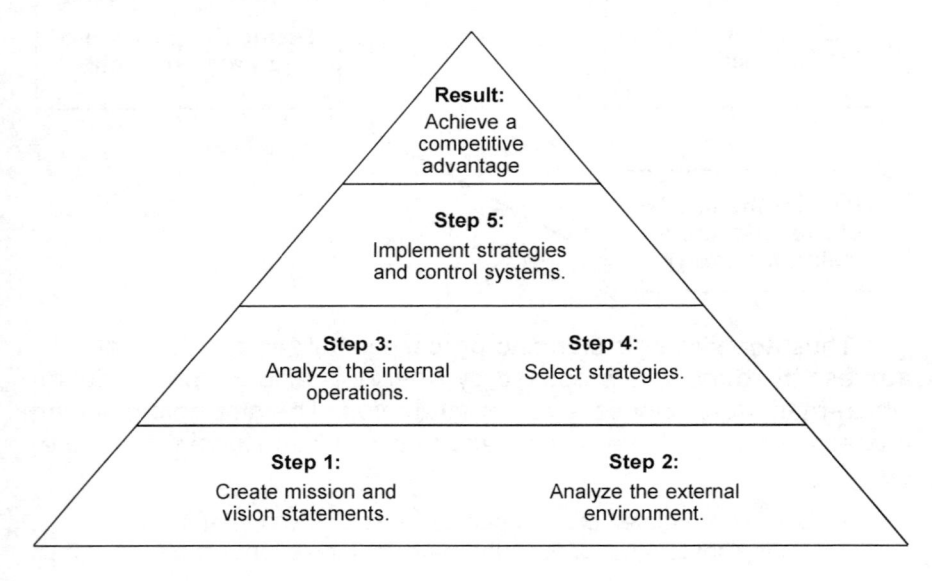

Result:
Achieve a competitive advantage

Step 5: Implement strategies and control systems.

Step 3: Analyze the internal operations.

Step 4: Select strategies.

Step 1: Create mission and vision statements.

Step 2: Analyze the external environment.

Competitive Advantage

Some experts contend that competitive advantage is really a strategy to give an organization a distinct advantage over its competition. According to Michael Porter in his 1985 work *Competitive Advantage,* an organization must select a competitive strategy in order to successfully perform at an above-average profitability level because no firm can be all things to all people. Porter proposed three competitive strategy options: cost leadership, a differentiation strategy, and a focus strategy.

Cost leadership is a strategy in which an organization attempts to be the lowest-cost producer in its industry. A firm can obtain a low-cost advantage through efficient operations, economies of scale, technological innovation, low-cost labor, or preferential access to raw materials.

A *differentiation* strategy occurs when an organization attempts to distinguish itself from its industry competitors within a broad market. To achieve a differentiation strategy, an organization strives to obtain a unique position in the marketplace by emphasizing high quality, extraordinary service, an innovative product design, technological capability, or an unusually positive brand image. The key is that the unique position that the company is attempting to establish must be significantly different from its rivals to justify a price premium that exceeds the cost of differentiating.

A *focus* strategy is when an organization wants to establish an advantage in a narrow market segment. The focus strategy utilizes either a cost advantage or a differentiation approach aimed at a narrow market segment.

In order to achieve long-term success, an organization must sustain its competitive advantage. Tactics that organizations use to achieve a long-run competitive advantage include establishing barriers to entry, such as patents, copyrights, trademarks, or economies of scale. Firms sometimes lower prices to gain market share, tie up suppliers with exclusive contracts, or lobby Congress to impose trade restrictions designed to limit foreign competition.

Underlying Porter's three competitive strategies are the generic building blocks of competitive advantage, as described by Charles W. L. Hill and Gareth R. Jones (1998):

1. Superior efficiency is about converting inputs into outputs. Inputs are the basic factors of production, such as labor, land, capital, management, and technological know-how. Outputs are the goods and services that an organization produces. The more efficiently an organization can convert inputs into outputs, the higher the productivity level of that organization. The organization with the highest level of productivity in an industry typically has the lowest costs of production, and therefore gains a competitive advantage.

2. The impact of superior product quality on competitive advantage is twofold. First, providing high-quality products increases the value of those products in the eyes of the consumer (target market) that allows the firm to charge a higher price. The second impact of high quality on competitive advantage comes from the greater efficiency and lower unit cost it brings.

3. Superior innovation is the most important of the building blocks of competitive advantage. Innovation can be defined as anything new or novel about the way a company operates or about the products it produces. Innovative organizations provide consumers with products that are not available from other firms. That lack of availability allows the organization to charge a premium for its product. In addition, innovative organizations can build brand loyalty, which makes it more difficult for rivals to gain market share.

4. Superior customer service or responsiveness is achieved by identifying and satisfying the needs of the consumers (target market) better than any other organization. Superior customer responsiveness includes such activities as quality, customization, response time, design, and superior service before and after the sale.

Organizations that focus on the building blocks of competitive advantage increase the probability of improving the firm's bottom line. When everything else is all said and done, increasing the bottom line *is* the bottom line!

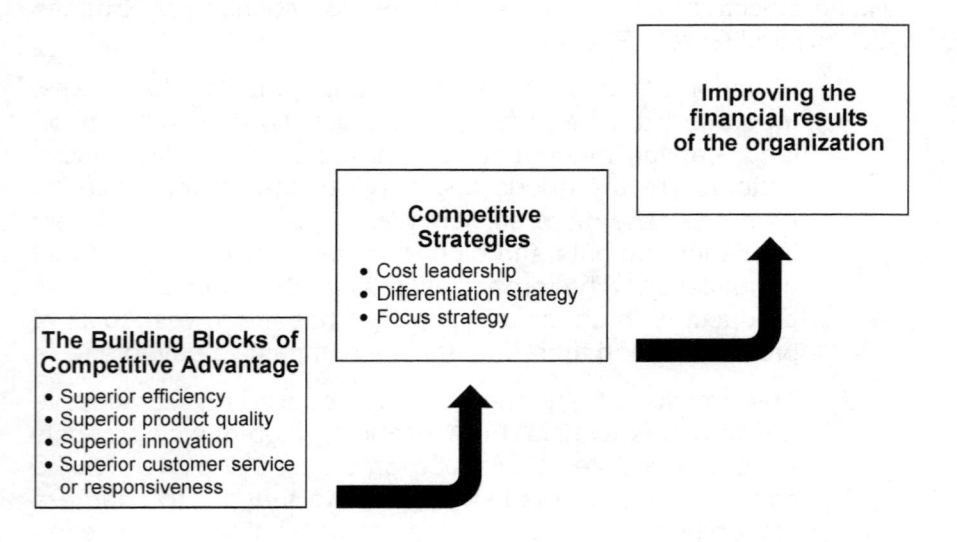

The Building Blocks of Competitive Advantage
- Superior efficiency
- Superior product quality
- Superior innovation
- Superior customer service or responsiveness

Competitive Strategies
- Cost leadership
- Differentiation strategy
- Focus strategy

Improving the financial results of the organization

Output Value Creation and Competitive Advantage

Another important concept connected with the building blocks of competitive advantage is the notion of output value creation—the value of the product or service produced by an organization. An organization creates output value by developing a strategic plan that focuses on the building blocks of competitive advantage. This plan should address the needs of the target market and the employees. In this context, the target market will be specifically referred to as a group of people for which an organization designs, implements, and maintains a strategic plan intended to meet the needs of that group, resulting in mutually satisfying exchanges. The output value generated by an organization is measured by the equation **V = B/P** (the letter V represents value; B represents perceived and/or actual benefits; and P represents the price of the product). A higher output value as perceived by the target market increases the probability of gaining market share and improving profitability.

Output Value Creation and Putting Employees First

Lurking beneath the equation (**V = B/P**) is the ability of the workforce and individual employees to create product benefits in an efficient manner. Just like the portion of an iceberg that lies below the water, it is what's underneath the waterline that can be extremely dangerous; the ill-fated voyage of the *Titanic* will always serve to remind us of that. Thus, the lesson to be learned is that to enhance the output value-creation process, an organization needs to put its employees first. Here is how Thompson and Stickland (2003) put it:

> Organizations with a spirit of high performance typically are intensely people-oriented, and they reinforce their concern for individual employees on every conceivable occasion in every conceivable way. They treat employees with dignity and respect, train each employee thoroughly, encourage employees to use their own initiative and creativity in performing their work, set reasonable and clear performance standards, hold managers at every level responsible for developing the people who report to them, and grant

employees enough autonomy to stand out, excel, and contribute. Creating a results-oriented organizational culture generally entails making champions out of the people who turn in winning performances.

At its basic level, high performance essentially revolves around knowing how the abilities of each employee differ, and using that knowledge to increase the likelihood that any employee will consistently perform his or her job well. Employee job performance begins the "chain" of workplace activity that determines the level of productivity that a group or organization will eventually achieve. Productive environments at the group or organizational level are linked to and depend on the performance of each employee. Like any link in a chain, the productivity that a group or organization can achieve will only be as high as the weakest link in the chain of workplace activity. Group accomplishments and organizational productivity are a function of individual accomplishments and productivity.

Chain of Workplace Activity that Influences Productivity

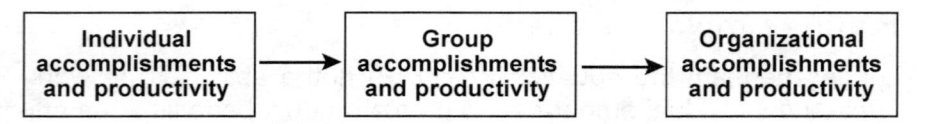

Individual accomplishments and productivity	→	Group accomplishments and productivity	→	Organizational accomplishments and productivity

(A group refers to a department or major function within an organization.)

Generally, how well an employee performs on the job will be reflective of the employee's intellectual and physical abilities, as well as the job fit between an employee's abilities and the job task. *Intellectual ability* refers to an employee's capability to do mental activities. The seven most frequently cited dimensions making up intellectual abilities are listed below, as explained by Stephen Robbins (2001):

1. **Number aptitude** is the ability to do speedy and accurate arithmetic.
2. **Verbal comprehension** is the ability to understand what is read or heard and the relationship between the words.

3. **Perceptual speed** is the ability to identify visual similarities and differences quickly and accurately.
4. **Inductive reasoning** is the ability to identify a logical sequence in a problem, and then to solve the problem.
5. **Deductive reasoning** is the ability to use logic and assess the implications of an argument.
6. **Spatial visualization** is the ability to imagine how an object would look if its position in space were changed.
7. **Memory** is the ability to retain and recall past experiences.

Physical ability refers to the stamina, dexterity, strength, and similar characteristics that are required to perform a task. The nine basic abilities involved in the performance of physical tasks are listed below, from the same source:

1. **Dynamic strength** is the ability to exert muscular force repeatedly or continuously over time.
2. **Trunk strength** is the ability to exert muscular strength using the trunk (particularly abdominal) muscles.
3. **Static strength** is the ability to exert force against external objects.
4. **Explosive strength** is the ability to expend a maximum of energy in one or a series of explosive acts.
5. **Extent flexibility** is the ability to move the trunk and back muscles as far as possible.
6. **Dynamic flexibility** is the ability to make rapid, repeated flexing movements.
7. **Body coordination** is the ability to coordinate the simultaneous actions of different parts of the body.
8. **Balance** is the ability to maintain equilibrium, despite forces pulling off-balance.
9. **Stamina** is the ability to continue maximum effort when prolonged effort is required over time.

Strategic Training: Putting Employees First

To maximize employee performance, you must match the intellectual and physical abilities of an employee to the job. When the employee ability–job match is out of equilibrium because the employee's abilities exceed or are not sufficient to perform the task, the performance level of the employee will be marginal, at best. Marginally performing employees result in under-performing groups and an unproductive, non-competitive organization.

The employee ability–job match is out of equilibrium when...

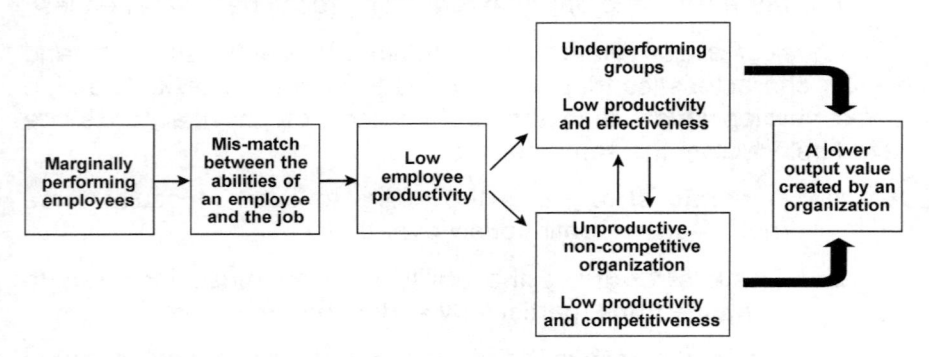

```
┌──────────────┐   ┌──────────────┐   ┌──────────────┐      ┌──────────────────┐
│ Marginally   │   │ Mis-match    │   │ Low          │      │ Underperforming  │
│ performing   │ → │ between the  │ → │ employee     │  ↗   │ groups           │
│ employees    │   │ abilities of │   │ productivity │      │ Low productivity │
│              │   │ an employee  │   │              │      │ and effectiveness│
│              │   │ and the job  │   │              │      └──────────────────┘
└──────────────┘   └──────────────┘   └──────────────┘            ↑ ↓
                                                          ┌──────────────────┐
                                                          │ Unproductive,    │
                                                          │ non-competitive  │
                                                          │ organization     │
                                                          │ Low productivity │
                                                          │ and competitiveness│
                                                          └──────────────────┘
                                                                 ↓
                                                   ┌────────────────────┐
                                                   │ A lower output     │
                                                   │ value created by an│
                                                   │ organization       │
                                                   └────────────────────┘
```

(A group refers to a department or major function within an organization.)

On the other hand, when the employee ability–job match is in equilibrium, an unproductive workplace can be transformed into a productive environment that generates a high output value. This transformation requires that the commitments to put employees first and provide quality training programs be linked to the strategic planning process. An organization that blends these commitments with the strategic planning process creates a work environment dedicated to enhancing the abilities and skills of their employees. Within this type of work environment, employee productivity is nourished and can grow. As employee productivity expands, output value increases.

Group and Organizational Success

```
┌─────────────┐   ┌─────────┐                ┌──────────────┐
│  Employee   │   │Employee │                │    Highly    │
│  abilities  │   │abilities│    ┌────────┐ ↗│productive and│
│ Intellectual│ → │   and   │ → │  High   │  │  competitive │         ┌──────────────┐
│  abilities  │   │ Job fit │   │employee │  │    groups    │⤵       │  A higher    │
│  Physical   │   │         │   │producti-│  └──────────────┘         │ output value │
│  abilities  │   │         │   │  vity   │       ↑ ↓                 │ created by an│
└─────────────┘   └─────────┘   └────────┘ ↘ ┌──────────────┐         │ organization │
                                              │  A highly    │⤴       └──────────────┘
                                              │productive and│
                                              │  competitive │
                                              │ organization │
                                              └──────────────┘
        ↑                    ↑                    ↑
┌─────────────────────────────────────────────────────────────────┐
│ Integrating the commitments to put employees first and provide  │
│    quality training programs within the strategic planning      │
│                           process                                │
└─────────────────────────────────────────────────────────────────┘
```

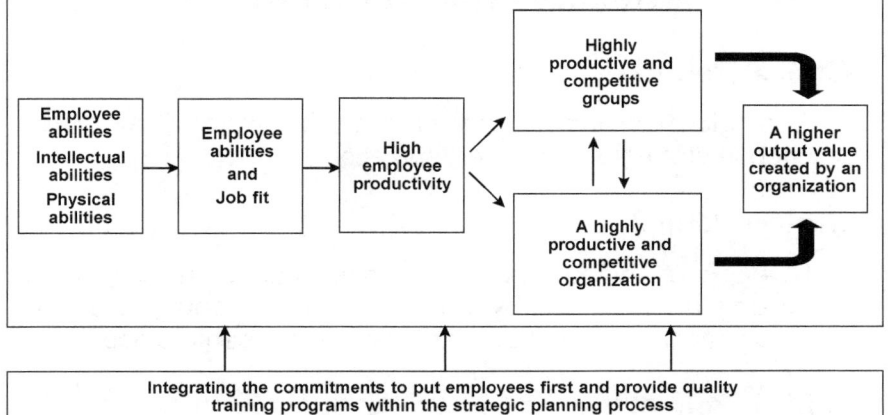

Putting employees first and providing quality training programs that are directly connected with the strategic objectives of an organization creates an environment within which the output value-creation process can flourish, just as long-overdue rain can transform a barren patch of land into a garden oasis.

How can an organization integrate its commitments to put employees first and provide quality training programs within the strategic planning process? That is the next part of our journey.

Critical Points in Chapter 2

Critical Point 1

Strategic planning is the process by which managers choose strategies for the organization.

Critical Point 2

Strategic planning should improve managerial decision making, as measured by the competitive advantage that an organization achieves over its rivals in the marketplace.

Critical Point 3

A competitive advantage is a strategy to position an organization in such a way that it will have a distinct advantage over its competition. There are three good competitive strategy options: cost leadership, differentiation strategy, and focus strategy.

Critical Point 4

The foundation for Michael Porter's competitive strategies are the generic building blocks of competitive advantage: superior efficiency, superior product quality, superior innovation, and superior customer service or responsiveness.

Critical Point 5

Another critical concept associated with the generic building blocks of competitive advantage is the notion of output value creation. Output value creation is measured by the equation ($V = B/P$), where V represents product value, B represents the perceived and/or actual benefits of the product, and P represents the price of the product.

Critical Point 6

A higher output value as perceived by the target market increases the probability of gaining market share and improving profitability. In this context, the target market is defined as a group of people for whom an organization designs, implements, and maintains a strategic plan.

Critical Point 7

Organizations that put employees first enhance the output value-creation process by improving the abilities of the employees, resulting in higher productivity.

Critical Point 8

Training critically impacts the abilities of an employee.

Critical Point 9

Integrating the dual commitments to put employees first and provide quality employee training programs within the strategic planning process eventually results in a higher output value.

Integrate: To bring together into a whole; to unify.

Integration: A combination and coordination of separate and diverse elements, functions, or units of an organization to promote a more complete or harmonious whole.

Chapter 3
A Deeper Journey into the Realm of Strategy Formulation

The Levels of Strategic Planning

As you may recall from Chapter 2, higher output value (as measured by the equation $V = B/P$) can be achieved if the commitments to put employees first and provide them with quality training are integrated within the strategic planning process. To better understand how to accomplish this integration, we need to take a deeper journey into the realm of strategy formulation.

Strategy formulation generally consists of four levels of planning: a corporate level, a business level, a functional level, and an operating level.

Corporate Strategy

The strategic emphasis at the corporate level is on six grand strategies:

1. Concentration on a single business
2. Vertical integration
3. Diversification
4. Strategic alliances
5. Restructuring or retrenchment
6. A combination strategy

Concentration on a Single Business. For many organizations, the appropriate corporate level strategy is to concentrate on competing successfully within the confines of a single business or industry or market.

Vertical Integration. Vertical integration is integrating the operations of an organization backward into the production of inputs or forward into the disposal of outputs. In other words, vertical integration refers to gaining control over the distribution channel by acquiring other organizations throughout the channel.

Diversification. The corporate strategy of diversification can be separated into two major categories: related and unrelated. *Related* *diversification* is diversification into new business activities that are linked to an organization's existing business activity or activities within the production process. Normally, these linkages are based on manufacturing, marketing, or technological commonalities. The production process is referred to as a "chain" of activities that an organization performs in order to transform inputs into outputs. *Unrelated diversification* is diversification into a new business area that has no obvious connection with any of the organization's existing areas.

Two common diversification techniques are mergers and acquisitions. A *merger* occurs when two organizations, usually of similar size, combine their resources to form a new organization. An *acquisition* occurs when a larger organization purchases a smaller one and incorporates the acquired organization's operations into its own.

There are three ways to determine whether or not an organization should diversify: Determine the attractiveness of the industry; determine the cost-of-entry into the industry; or perform the better-off analysis (the proposed diversified organization must be able to generate a higher output value). A diversification plan that passes only one or two of the tests is suspect.

Strategic Alliances. Strategic alliances are agreements between two or more organizations to share costs, risks, and benefits associated with developing new business projects or opportunities.

Restructuring or Retrenchment. Restructuring/retrenchment is a strategy characteristic of an organization that is reducing its size, usually in an environment of decline.

Combination Strategy. Finally, a combination strategy involves the simultaneous pursuit by an organization of two or more of the grand strategies.

Business Strategy

The primary objective of business-level strategy is to determine how each business unit is positioned against its rivals in the marketplace in order to achieve a competitive advantage. There are three generic business-level strategies (outlined earlier in the book):
1. Cost Leadership
2. Differentiation
3. Focus

Functional Strategy

Functional strategy uses a managerial game plan for running a major functional activity or process within a business unit, such as research and development, production, marketing, customer service, distribution, finance, human resources, and so on. At the core of functional-level strategy is the desire to improve the effectiveness of functional operations within an organization in order to attain superior efficiency, quality, innovation, and/or customer responsiveness.

Operating Strategy

Operating strategy concerns how to manage key, front-line operating units (plants, sales districts, distribution centers) and how to handle daily operating tasks with strategic significance (advertising campaigns, materials purchasing, inventory control, maintenance, shipping, and so forth). Operating strategies, while limited in scope, provide additional detail and completeness to functional strategies.

With strategy formulation occurring at four levels, the task of integrating the two commitments to put employees first and develop quality training programs into the strategic planning process becomes quite clear. The integration must occur *at each level of the strategic planning process* in order to generate a higher output value.

Strategic Training: Putting Employees First

The Integration Process

Strategic Planning	Organizational commitment to:	A higher output value created by an organization
Corporate level Business level Functional level Operating level	Put employees first and Provide quality training programs	

In sum, the strategic planning process at all levels (corporate, business, functional, and operating) will only be as good as the quality of the individuals developing and implementing the strategies. There's no escaping the fact that the most valuable assets of an organization are the people who work in the organization. Strategic plans that generate superior output value require well-trained employees, and well-trained employees are nurtured and developed through quality training. Quality training programs equate to quality employees. Quality employees are the ultimate source of organizational success. Organizations with a type "A" or "B" culture understand this truism and consequently tend to generate higher output value.

Group and Organizational Success

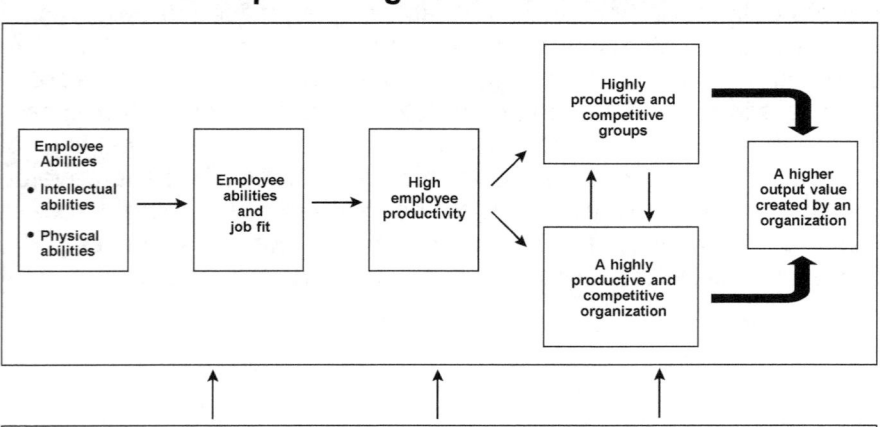

Employee Abilities
- Intellectual abilities
- Physical abilities

→ Employee abilities and job fit → High employee productivity →

- Highly productive and competitive groups
- A highly productive and competitive organization

→ A higher output value created by an organization

Organizations with a type "A" or "B" culture integrate the organizational principles of putting employees first and providing quality training programs throughout each level of the strategic planning process (corporate, business, functional, operating).

An organization with a higher output value will outperform an organization with a lower value. However, the quest to create output value is further complicated by the problem of scarcity, because the resources of an organization are limited. Scarcity forces organizational decision makers to make decisions regarding resource allocations. The training function, like every other function within an organization, is not immune to the time and financial constraints faced by an organization. It is this dilemma that we will now explore.

Strategic Training: Putting Employees First

Critical Points in Chapter 3

Critical Point 1

Strategic planning occurs at four levels: a corporate level, a business level, a functional level, and an operating level.

Critical Point 2

Integrating the commitment to put employees first and provide quality training programs must be done at each level of the strategic planning process in order to generate a higher output value.

Critical Point 3

Organizations with a type "A" or "B" culture integrate organizational commitments to put employees first, and provide quality training programs throughout each level of the strategic planning process, and therefore generate a higher output value.

Critical Point 4

Creating output value is further complicated by the problem of scarcity, because organizational resources are limited. Therefore, decisions must be made on resource allocations.

> The important thing for demonstrating training value is to avoid any "nice to have." In this era of limited means, stick with the "need to have."
>
> – Howard McCarley

Chapter 4
Scarcity

Scarcity: Potential Training Content Versus Usable Training Content

We said in Chapter 1 that the Financial Status Model of Organizational Culture (FSMOC) provides a methodology for analyzing the culture and financial performance of an organization. The people are the basis of the FSMOC model; without quality employees, the output value generated by an organization will wither, and mediocrity will become the norm. An organization overrun by mediocrity is destined to under-perform, trapped within a "D" or "F" organizational culture. Contrast that to "A" or "B" cultures, which have highly productive work environments. However, even these organizations are limited by scarce resources; they must account for organizational constraints, such as time restrictions and personnel and budgetary/financial limitations.

Every organization encounters time and financial constraints. As a result of organizational constraints, organizational decision makers are forced to make resource allocation decisions, including how much training can be provided to the employees.

Organizational constraints tend to limit the level of training offered. The challenge organizations face is to provide *quality* training programs with the resources they have. Offering too much training wastes already-limited organizational resources, whereas too little training will hinder the ability of an organization to generate output value. Ultimately, the type and level of training an employee is given is going to be based on the strategic goals and objectives of an organization, its culture, and its constraints. A high-leverage training approach links adult learning theory with the strategic objectives of an organization, and thus will be utilized in the Strategic Training of Employees Model (STEM). However, the model is much more than the concepts associated with high-leverage training. It can help an organization strategically increase its output value, even with reduced resources.

When resources are scarce, we must draw a distinction between potential training content and usable training content. *Potential* training content exists in a theoretical world where scarcity does not exist and the organization can devote an unlimited amount of resources toward training. *Usable* training content is firmly embedded in the practical, day-to-day environment where organizational resources are scarce and allocation decisions must be made.

Scarcity and the Level of Training

Developing a training model that captures the reality of scarce organizational resources is important. American companies spend more than $50 billion per year on training, but the effectiveness of that training is questionable. Why? As Christer Idhammar points out, much of the training in the United States is commonly referred to as the "follow Joe" type: New employees are teamed with experienced employees, and the new employees are expected to learn on the job. However, not all the necessary information gets passed along from experienced employees to the new ones. For instance, let's suppose that Joe, an experienced worker, is responsible for teaching Mike, a new employee. Joe might only possess a certain percentage of the knowledge he should be aware of. In addition, Joe might not teach Mike everything he knows, keeping some skills to himself because of pride and/or job security. However, even if Joe teaches Mike everything that he knows, Mike might not be able to remember all of it.

The type and level of the training that an organization ultimately provides is determined by the strategic desires of an organization and its culture, which will influence the level of constraints. An organization with a type "A" or a type "B" culture devotes more resources to developing the abilities of its employees, and therefore the level of constraints will be lower. An organization with a "D" or an "F" culture allocates fewer resources for employee training and development, so the level of constraints will be higher. The level of training an organization will provide can be illustrated by Finch and Crunkilton's Training Content Equation and the Strategic Training Content Equation.

Training Content Equation

$$UTC = PTC - C$$

UTC = usable training content; *PTC* = potential training content; *C* = organizational constraints

Strategic Training Content Equation

$$USTC = PTC - NSTC - C$$

$USTC$ = usable strategic training content; PTC = potential training content; $NSTC$ = non-strategic training content; C = organizational constraints

Note: Usable strategic training content can alternatively stand for employee training and career development that is associated with achieving strategic organizational goals.

$$USTC = SET + SCD$$

$USTC$ = usable strategic training content; SET = strategic employee training; SCD = strategic career development

Therefore, the strategic training content equation can be written as:

$$SET + SCD = PTC - NSTC - C$$

SET = strategic employee training; SCD = strategic career development; PTC = potential training content; $NSTC$ = non-strategic training content; C = constraints

What the Training Content Equation and the Strategic Training Content Equation clearly illustrate is that scarcity imposes restrictions on training content. Since scarcity can never be completely eliminated, the STEM model provides organizational decision makers and human resource practitioners with a systematic and practical mechanism for effectively and efficiently allocating training content, given the reality of scarcity.

Scarcity drives resource allocation decisions, including the level of training provided to employees	→	The STEM model provides a systematic and practical mechanism for allocating training content, given the problem of scarcity

Like most models, the roots of the STEM model are embedded in the relevant academic literature. In this case, that literature includes the economic research relating to the development of human capital, as well as the literature pertaining to the learning process, with an emphasis on the implications for organizational training.

Economic Literature and Human Capital

In a seminal 1962 work, Gary Becker laid the foundation for the study of human capital acquisition when he distinguished between *general* human capital and *specific* human capital. General human capital has multiple uses, and is therefore portable; specific human capital is useful in a narrow line of work, and therefore has limited portability. Accordingly, general training is basically an investment in human capital to increase an employee's overall productivity, and it can be transferred to any employment situation. Specific training only increases worker productivity in the job area where the training occurred. Becker concluded that within a perfectly competitive market, any general human capital formulation will be financed by the individual; any specific human capital acquisition will be shared by individuals and firms.

After Becker's work was published, economic research workplace analysis examined physical capital issues. Recently, however, several researchers have begun investigating various topics relating to human capital development. Economic research serves as a valuable reminder of the tug of war between the need to provide employee training and the associated costs. Most organizations (with the exception of academically oriented entities such as schools, colleges, and universities) do not exist for the sole purpose of educating their employees, so there will be some internal debate regarding the level and degree of training, a dilemma that once again focuses attention on the concepts of potential and usable training content as outlined by Finch and Crunkilton.

Learning Theories and Training Implications

Scott Barnett, president and CEO of the Bubba Gump Shrimp Company, believes that training needs to provide for the different learning styles of all employees. Learning is a relatively permanent change in human capabilities that is not a result of growth processes. These capabilities are related to specific learning outcomes (verbal information, intellectual skills, motor skills, attitudes, and cognitive strategies). Several learning theories can be utilized to provide a foundation for understanding how a trainee is motivated to learn.

Reinforcement theory emphasizes that people are motivated to perform or avoid certain behaviors because of past outcomes that have resulted from those behaviors. From a training perspective, reinforcement theory suggests that for learners to acquire knowledge, change their behavior, or modify skills, the trainer needs to identify what outcomes the learner perceives as being positive (or negative). Trainers then need to link these outcomes to learners who need or want to acquire knowledge or skills, or change behaviors.

Social learning theory suggests that learners first watch others who act as models. In a training scenario, a group of trainees can be presented with models of effective behaviors (e.g., serving customers, performing managerial analyses) and told about the relationship between these desirable behaviors and their various consequences (such as praise, promotions, or customer satisfaction). Trainees then rehearse the behaviors and consequences, building cognitive maps that intensify the links and set the stage for future behaviors. The learning impact occurs when the subject tries the behavior and experiences a positive result.

Goal-setting theory implies that establishing and committing to specific and challenging goals can influence an individual's behavior. From a training perspective, setting goals can help an individual identify the specific outcomes that should be achieved from the training.

Need theories (Maslow's Hierarchy of Needs, Alderfer's ERG Theory, Herzberg's Dual-Structure Theory, and David McClelland's Need Theory) assume that need deficiencies cause behavior. Need theories suggest that to motivate learning, trainers should identify trainees' needs and communicate how training program content relates to fulfilling those needs.

Expectancy theory implies that an individual's behavior is a function of three factors (expectancy, instrumentality, and valence). The *expectancy* factor refers to an individual's belief that the effort will lead to a particular performance level; that the performance level is associated with a particular outcome (instrumentality factor); and that the outcome is valued by the individual (valence factor).

From a training perspective, expectancy theory suggests that learning is most likely to occur when employees believe they can learn the content of the program (expectancy); when learning is linked to an outcome, such as better job performance, a salary increase, or peer recognition (instrumentality); and when employees value the outcomes.

Adult Learning Theory (Andragogy) and Implications for Workplace Training

Can you recall the last time you participated in a training session that provided useful information? When you think back to that training experience, what were the factors that made the session so valuable? The training programs I personally found most worthwhile were well organized; the material that was being presented related to my job; and the presenter provided numerous demonstrations or examples. What was critical for me in order to understand the material, however, was that I had an opportunity to practice what was being discussed. These are probably the same factors you consider important for creating a positive training environment. Educational psychologists developed the theory of adult learning, *andragogy,* when they began to understand the importance of adult learning (up until that point, pedagogy dominated the research literature on education.) Malcolm Knowles (1990) is most frequently associated with adult learning theory. Some conclusions or recommendations regarding adult learning theory for workplace training are summarized here:

Learning in the Workplace

Employees learn best when they understand the objective of the training program. The training objective should comprise three components: an explanation of what the employee is expected to do (performance); a statement of the quality or level of performance that is acceptable (criterion); and a declaration of the conditions under which the trainee is expected to perform the desired outcome (conditions).

(continued)

Learning in the Workplace (concluded)

> **Employees tend to learn better when the training is linked to their current job experiences,** because this enhances the meaningfulness of the training. The training experience can be further enhanced by providing trainees with opportunities to choose their practice strategy as well as other characteristics of the learning situation.
>
> **Employees learn best when they have the opportunity to practice.** The trainer should identify and explain three things: what the trainees will be doing when practicing the objectives (performance); the criteria for attainment of the objective; and the conditions under which the practice session(s) will be conducted.
>
> **Employees need feedback.** To be effective, the feedback should focus on specific behaviors, and be provided as soon as possible following the behavior.
>
> **Employees learn by observing and imitating the actions of a model.** For the model to be effective, the desired behaviors or skills need to be clearly specified, and the model should have characteristics (such as age or position) similar to those of the target audience. After observing the model, trainees should have the opportunity to reproduce the skills and behaviors shown by the model.
>
> **Employees need the training program to be properly coordinated and arranged.** Good coordination ensures that trainees are not distracted by an uncomfortable room or poorly organized materials or anything else that might interfere with learning.

The linking of adult learning theory with the strategic objectives of the organization is referred to as "high-leverage" training. High-leverage training helps establish a corporate culture in which continuous learning is encouraged. Continuous learning requires employees to understand the entire work system, including the relationships among their jobs, their work units, and the company. Employees are expected to acquire new skills and knowledge, apply them on the job, and share this information with other employees.

Strategic Training: Putting Employees First

A model that merges high-leverage training with various concepts from other learning theories while accounting for constraints would provide a useful methodology to help an organization achieve the highest possible output value, given the realization that the problem of scarcity will always exist to some extent for all organizations. STEM is that model.

Creating the Highest Possible Output Value, Given the Reality of Scarcity

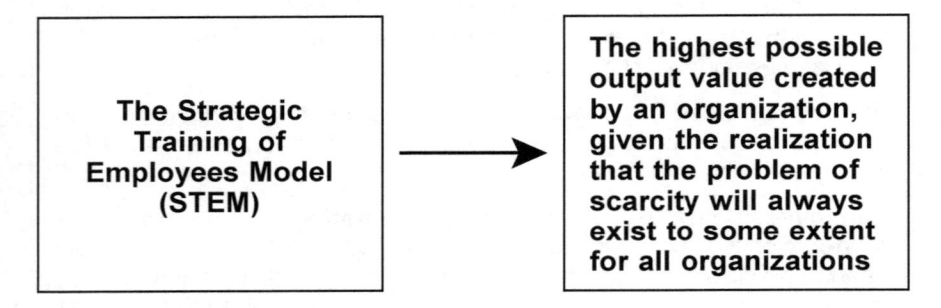

The Strategic Training of Employees Model (STEM)	⟶	**The highest possible output value created by an organization, given the realization that the problem of scarcity will always exist to some extent for all organizations**

Critical Points in Chapter 4

Critical Point 1

Because of scarcity, the type and level of training an organization decides to provide can be illustrated by the Finch and Crunkilton's Training Content Equation, further clarified by the Strategic Training Content Equation.

The Training Content Equation

$$UTC = PTC - C$$

UTC = usable training content; PTC = potential training content; C = organizational constraints

The Strategic Training Content Equation

$$SET + SCD = PTC - NSTC - C$$

SET = strategic employee training; SCD = strategic career development; PTC = potential training content; $NSTC$ = non-strategic training content; C = organizational constraints

Critical Point 2

The STEM model provides a practical methodology for designing specific training and career development programs that relate to the strategic objectives of an organization, while accounting for organizational constraints.

Critical Point 3

By utilizing the STEM model, an organization will be able to generate the highest possible output value, given the realization that the problem of scarcity will always exist to some extent for all organizations.

Part II:
The Strategic Training of Employees Model (STEM)

Life is like a great carpet. Seen from one side of a loom, it makes no sense. It has no shape, no logic. Just hundreds of strands of wool hanging loosely here and there. But seen from the other side, everything can be understood. The pattern becomes clear. There are no loose bits of wool. Just order.

– Philip Kerr

Chapter 5
An Overview of the Strategic Training of Employees Model (STEM)

In Larry Millett's book *Sherlock Holmes and the Red Demon,* Sherlock Holmes is asked the following question:

"Now, Mr. Holmes, what will you need to begin your investigation?"

Holmes replied, "The facts. They are the foundation of all that will follow..."

In Part I of this book, we unearthed the facts regarding organizational performance and how to generate output value.

In Parts II and III, we will examine the framework of the Strategic Training of Employees Model (STEM) and show how the model can be used to overcome many of the major training problems or challenges that managers encounter today.

In their never-ending quest to improve performance, organizations chase after the most-recent technological breakthroughs or the latest marketing techniques or the "hottest" trends in management or finance theory the same way puppies race in circles trying to catch their tails. After all that frantic scrambling around, what tends to emerge from those efforts are short-term cost reductions and momentary spikes in some numbers on quarterly accounting reports—no long-term solutions to organizational competitiveness and success.

Steady, long-term competitiveness requires an organization to be committed to putting employees first and developing quality training programs that are linked to its strategic objectives. Without a true commitment to the employees at all levels throughout an organization, the journey to enhance organizational performance will be an elusive adventure. Quality employees equate to organizational success. Unqualified and poorly trained employees equate to organizational failure.

The American Society for Training and Development's 2004 State of the Industry Report says this: "Organizations that really get the link between learning and performance increase efforts to align learning with business goals, target learning resources at mission-critical competencies, and measure both the effectiveness of learning and the efficiency of the learning organization in delivering improved performance outcomes."

The skills and abilities of the employees drive organizational performance. Any organization can take steps to develop its employees not only to increase their productivity, but also to keep up with the changing needs of the marketplace *if* they have access to quality training.

Certified trainers such as Christine Benak are convinced that the employees are the key to organizational success. "Take care of your employees and they will take care of your customers," Benak advises. "Train your employees well and they will provide better customer service." Training will, however, have to be effective and efficient: the STEM model helps an organization design quality employee training and development programs (with limited resources) that focus on achieving the strategic objectives of an organization. When you efficiently allocate training content (as well as dollars), you improve the output value of the product that it brings to the marketplace.

The Basic Structure of the Strategic Training of Employees Model (STEM)

The model we are suggesting here consists of three levels: a macro-organizational training level, a micro-organizational training level, and an implementation, feedback, and evaluation level.

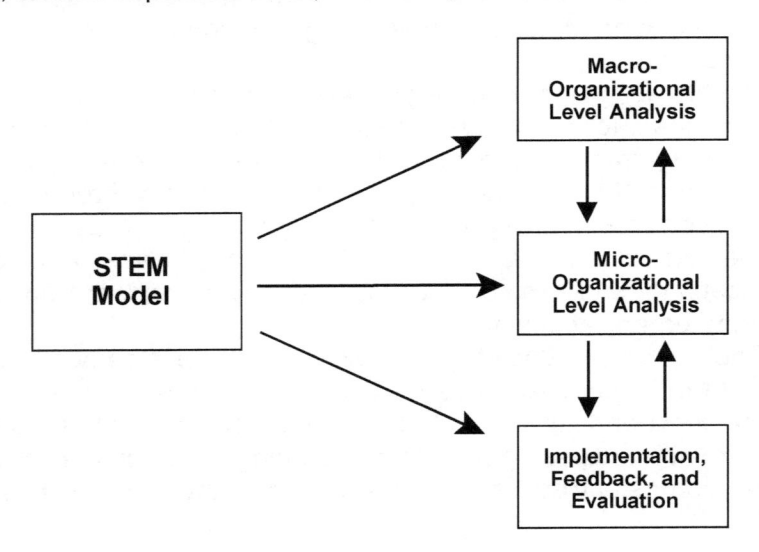

The Macro-Organizational Training Level

At the macro-organizational level, the strategic objectives that have been formulated by management are integrated with the training process. As we have said, strategic planning must occur at all four levels (corporate, business, functional, and operating). The training function must be linked to all four levels as well, because the output value that an organization generates will increase when the skills and abilities of the employees match the job tasks that are required to accomplish the strategic objectives of an organization. The director of training must be intimately involved in strategy formulation to ensure that the strategic planning process and the training function are seamlessly connected.

Analysis at the Macro-Organizational Training Level

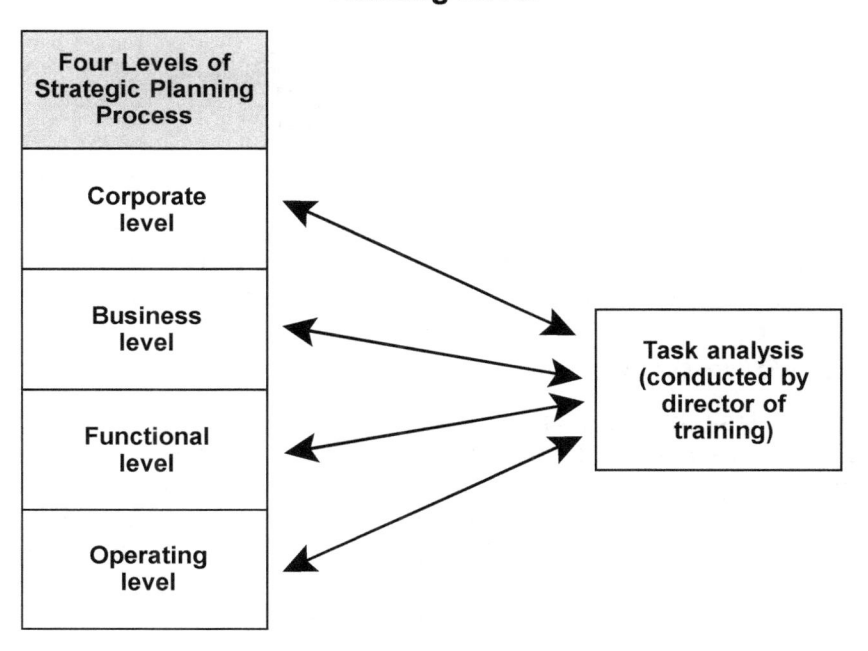

Four Levels of Strategic Planning Process	
Corporate level	←
Business level	← → Task analysis (conducted by director of training)
Functional level	← →
Operating level	←

From a macro-organizational perspective, linking the strategic objectives of an organization (at all four levels) with the abilities of the employees (by utilizing a task analysis) is a key determinant of output value.

In task analysis, the duties and tasks are used to identify the knowledge, skills, and abilities required to adequately perform a particular job. A task analysis generally consists of four steps:

1. Determine the jobs to be analyzed.
2. Make a preliminary list of the tasks involved to perform a job.
3. Validate or confirm the preliminary task list.
4. Identify the knowledge, skills, and abilities that are necessary to perform the job.

The Role of a Task Analysis in the STEM Model

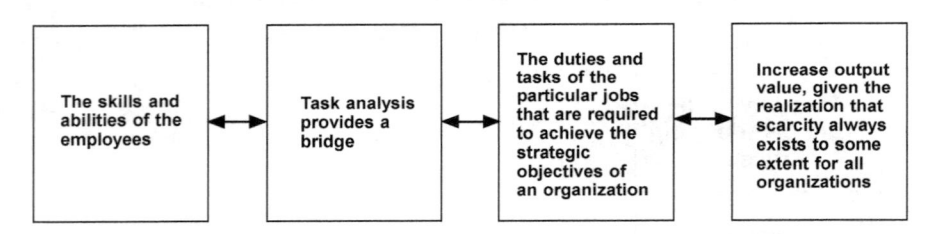

The skills and abilities of the employees	⟷	Task analysis provides a bridge	⟷	The duties and tasks of the particular jobs that are required to achieve the strategic objectives of an organization	⟷	Increase output value, given the realization that scarcity always exists to some extent for all organizations

Task analysis allows the skills and abilities of the employees to be matched with the duties and tasks of the specific jobs that are required to achieve the organization's strategic objectives.

The Micro-Organizational Training Level

After a task analysis is completed, the organization can begin developing employee training programs that are based on the list of jobs deemed necessary to support the strategic objectives established by management, as well as the tasks and skills required to perform each of these jobs. This information is then used to target specific employees for training, and then to design training content that will assist those employees in performing their jobs.

When determining training content, the "four Ps" approach (product, place, promotion, and price), first popularized in 1960 by E. Jerome McCarthy, will be used to provide a concise and practical framework for guiding training content decisions. This approach commonly used in marketing (also referred to as the "marketing mix") is defined as the set of controllable variables that a firm blends to produce the response it wants.

In our model, the product is the training content that will be provided; the place is the set of location factors regarding training; the promotion element refers to how information that pertains to training is communicated; and finally, the price refers to any costs associated with providing training.

Analysis at the Micro-Organizational Training Level

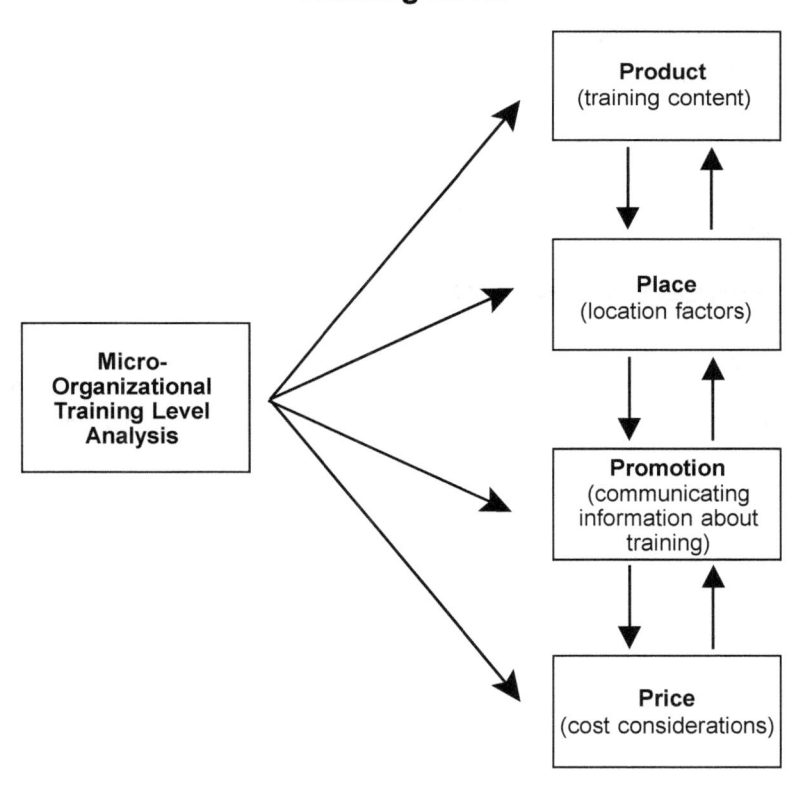

```
Micro-Organizational Training Level Analysis
    ├──▶ Product (training content)
    ├──▶ Place (location factors)
    ├──▶ Promotion (communicating information about training)
    └──▶ Price (cost considerations)
```

Once specific training programs have been developed, the final analysis level can begin: to implement, obtain feedback, and evaluate each training program.

The Strategic Training of Employees Model (STEM)

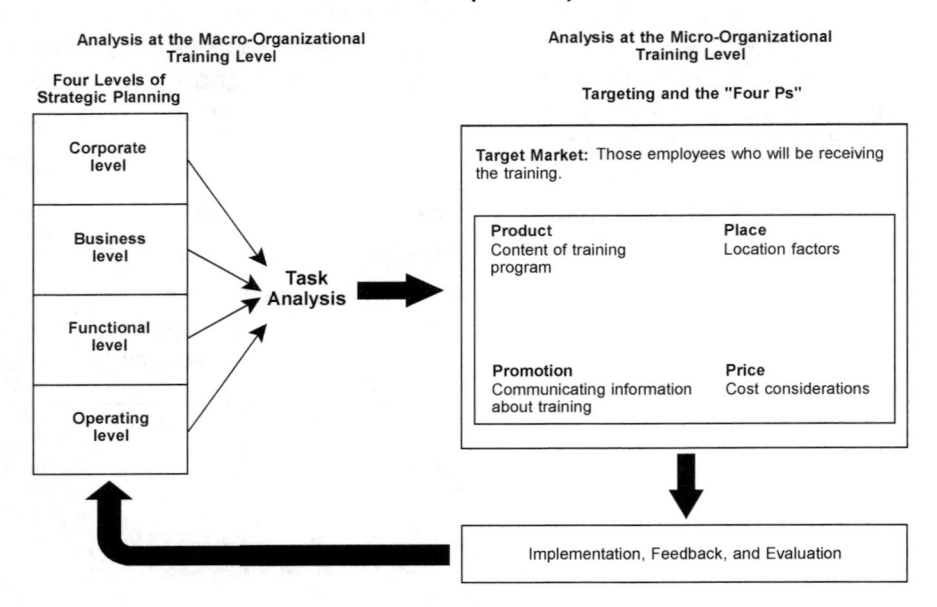

Analysis at the Macro-Organizational Training Level

Four Levels of Strategic Planning

- Corporate level
- Business level
- Functional level
- Operating level

Analysis at the Micro-Organizational Training Level

Targeting and the "Four Ps"

Target Market: Those employees who will be receiving the training.

Product — Content of training program

Place — Location factors

Promotion — Communicating information about training

Price — Cost considerations

Task Analysis

Implementation, Feedback, and Evaluation

The next chapters provide further details about how the STEM model can be used to design training and career development programs that will assist an organization in creating the highest possible output value.

An Overview of the Strategic Training of Employees Model

Critical Points in Chapter 5

Critical Point 1

Quality training equates to quality employees, which equates to organizational success in the marketplace. Organizations with type "A" or "B" cultures truly understand this.

Critical Point 2

Despite the importance of training, all organizations (including those with type "A" or "B" cultures) face constraints because of scarcity. Therefore, training and all other organizational functions must be conducted in an effective and efficient manner.

Critical Point 3

The Strategic Training of Employees Model (STEM) effectively and efficiently allocates training content by focusing on the strategic objectives of an organization, while accounting for constraints.

Critical Point 4

The STEM model consists of three levels: a macro-organizational level, a micro-organizational level, and an implementation, feedback, and evaluation level.

Critical Point 5

At the macro-organizational training level, the strategic objectives at the corporate, business, functional, and operating levels are integrated with the training function.

Critical Point 6

The director of training should assume a critical role in the strategic planning process to ensure that the abilities of the employees match the job tasks that are required to accomplish the strategic objectives of an organization.

Critical Point 7

A task analysis is a human resources process by which the abilities of an employee can be matched to the characteristics of the jobs that must be performed to accomplish the strategic objectives established by management.

Critical Point 8

At the micro-organizational training level, the training function becomes a matter of targeting specific employees for training, and then designing training content that will assist those employees in performing their jobs.

Critical Point 9

Product, place, promotion, and price will all be used to develop specific training programs.

Critical Point 10

Once specific training programs have been developed, the final level of the Strategic Training of Employees Model is to implement, obtain feedback, and evaluate each training program.

> Identifying the target market is a prerequisite for crafting specific training programs.

Chapter 6
Task Analysis and Targeting

The end product of a task analysis is a list of the jobs that must be performed to support the strategic objectives of an organization, and the knowledge, skills, and abilities associated with each of those jobs. The jobs included in the task analysis can be described in general terms: senior executives, upper-level managers, middle managers, lower-level managers, supervisory employees, and non-managerial employees. They can also be characterized in a more precise manner (i.e., job descriptions). A *job description* is a statement spelling out the tasks involved in a given job, as well as the job conditions.

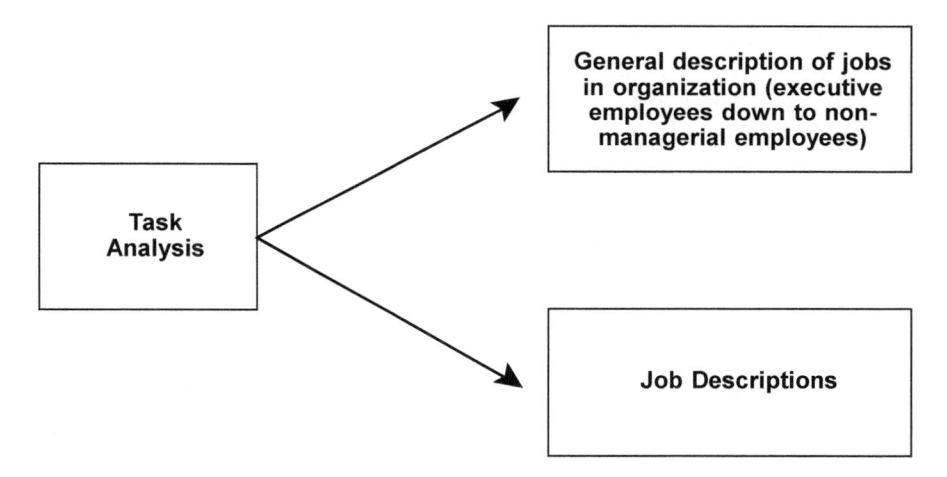

```
                    ┌─────────────────────────────┐
                    │ General description of jobs │
                    │ in organization (executive  │
              ┌────▶│ employees down to non-      │
              │     │ managerial employees)       │
┌──────────┐  │     └─────────────────────────────┘
│   Task   │──┤
│ Analysis │  │     ┌─────────────────────────────┐
└──────────┘  └────▶│      Job Descriptions       │
                    └─────────────────────────────┘
```

Once you do a task analysis, you are ready to target the employees who must be trained.

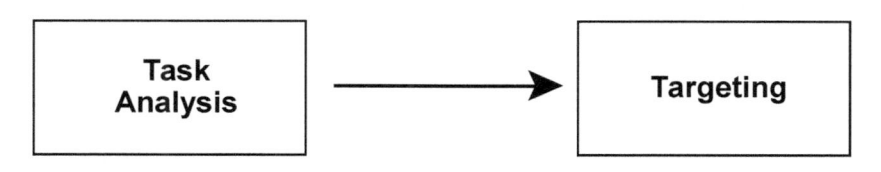

```
┌──────────┐          ┌──────────┐
│   Task   │ ───────▶ │Targeting │
│ Analysis │          │          │
└──────────┘          └──────────┘
```

73

The targeting of employees for training has its roots grounded in two marketing principles described here by Philip Kotler and Gary Armstrong (1991):

> **The marketing concept** holds that achieving organizational goals depends on determining the needs and wants of target markets and delivering the desired satisfactions more effectively and efficiently than do competitors.
>
> **A target market** is a set of buyers sharing common needs or characteristics that the company decides to serve.

From those two marketing ideas come two fundamental training factors:

> **The training concept.** Achievement of an organization's strategic goals for training and career development is directly related to whether or not an organization first determines the needs of an employee target market and then delivers the desired training in an effective and efficient manner.
>
> **The employee target market.** An employee or a set of employees who will be targeted or selected for training.

Once an employee target market has been identified and targeted or selected, the training process becomes a matter of designing effective and efficient training programs to ensure that the knowledge, skills, and abilities of the employee(s) match those necessary for success in the jobs that must be performed to support the strategic objectives of the organization.

In the next chapter, we will show how product, place, promotion, and price can be used to develop specific training content.

Task Analysis, Targeting, and the Design of Training Programs

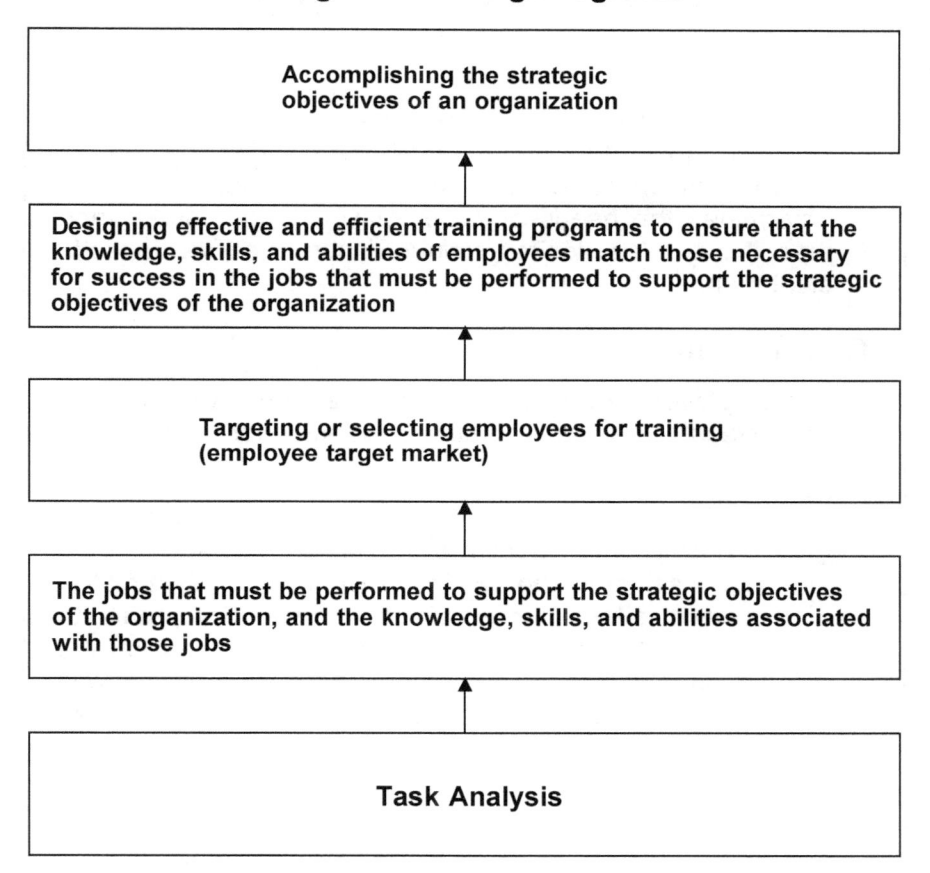

Accomplishing the strategic objectives of an organization

↑

Designing effective and efficient training programs to ensure that the knowledge, skills, and abilities of employees match those necessary for success in the jobs that must be performed to support the strategic objectives of the organization

↑

Targeting or selecting employees for training (employee target market)

↑

The jobs that must be performed to support the strategic objectives of the organization, and the knowledge, skills, and abilities associated with those jobs

↑

Task Analysis

Critical Points in Chapter 6

Critical Point 1

The Training Concept: Achievement of an organization's strategic goals for training and career development is directly related to whether or not the organization first determines the needs of an employee target market and then delivers the desired training in an effective and efficient manner.

Critical Point 2

The employee target market refers to an employee or set of employees who will be targeted or selected for training.

Critical Point 3

Once an employee target market has been identified and targeted or selected, the training process becomes a matter of designing effective and efficient training programs to ensure that the knowledge, skills, and abilities of the employees match those necessary for success in the jobs that must be performed to support the strategic objectives of the organization.

Critical Point 4

Product, place, price, and promotion factors will be used to develop specific training programs.

Task Analysis and Targeting

This diagram illustrates the complete STEM model:

The Strategic Training of Employees Model (STEM) with Task Analysis and Targeting Details

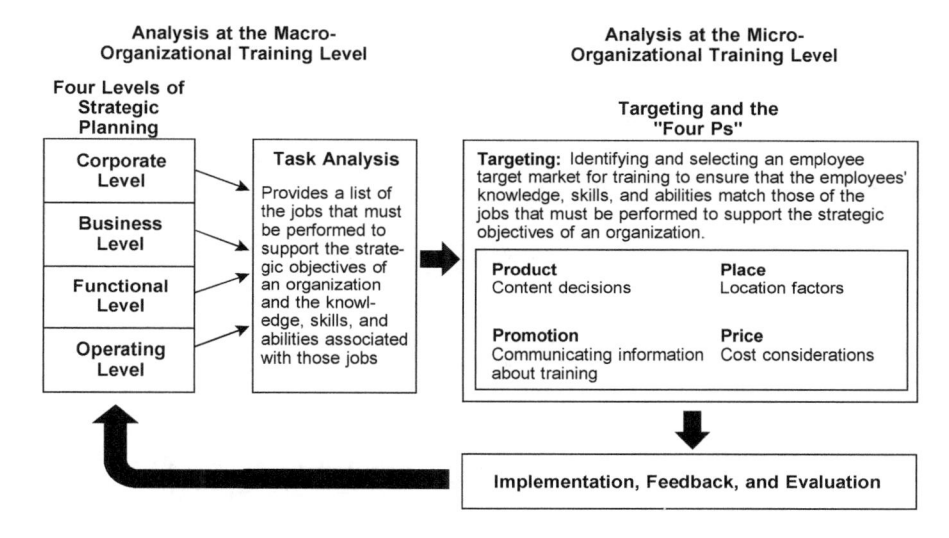

Analysis at the Macro-Organizational Training Level

Four Levels of Strategic Planning
- Corporate Level
- Business Level
- Functional Level
- Operating Level

Task Analysis
Provides a list of the jobs that must be performed to support the strategic objectives of an organization and the knowledge, skills, and abilities associated with those jobs

Analysis at the Micro-Organizational Training Level

Targeting and the "Four Ps"

Targeting: Identifying and selecting an employee target market for training to ensure that the employees' knowledge, skills, and abilities match those of the jobs that must be performed to support the strategic objectives of an organization.

Product
Content decisions

Place
Location factors

Promotion
Communicating information about training

Price
Cost considerations

Implementation, Feedback, and Evaluation

> A well-designed product should satisfy a want or need in the marketplace.

Chapter 7
Training Content (Product)

Training content objectives should be based on the answers to these questions: What is the purpose of the training? What are the organizational constraints that will limit the training content? What content should be included in the training program? How should the content (product) be presented?

Product Content

Decisions based on the training objectives fall into these areas:
- Purpose of the training
- Organizational constraints
- Specific training content
- Presentation options

Product Content Decisions

Training is not the same as career development. *Training* typically provides employees with specific skills or helps to correct deficiencies in the performance of an employee. Career development is about providing employees with the abilities an organization will need in the future. Keep this in mind when you identify the reasons why you are going to provide employee training.

Enhancing the skills of an employee might mean improving his or her basic reading and writing abilities, technological know-how, interpersonal communication, or problem-solving abilities, and possibly providing ethics training. Mentoring, coaching, job rotation, and tuition assistance are all part of career development training.

A task analysis helps you make sure that the training and career development necessary to accomplish strategic objectives will be effective; it provides you with a list of the jobs that must be performed to support the strategic objectives of an organization and the knowledge, skills, and abilities associated with those jobs.

Task Analysis: The Link Between Organizational Strategy and Training

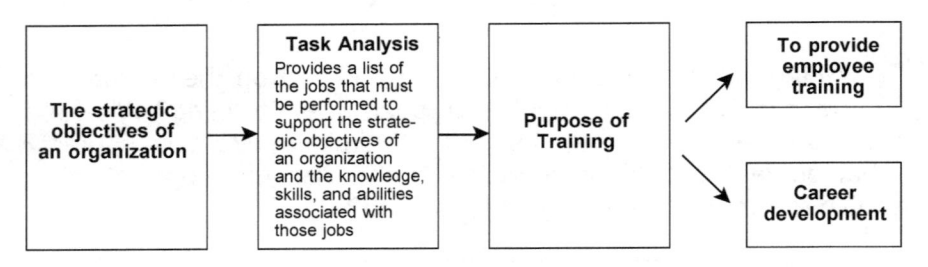

```
[The strategic objectives of an organization] → [Task Analysis: Provides a list of the jobs that must be performed to support the strategic objectives of an organization and the knowledge, skills, and abilities associated with those jobs] → [Purpose of Training] → [To provide employee training] / [Career development]
```

The hiring and orientation of new employees also has profound ramifications for training. If the quality of new hires is high, less training will be required, and if it is low, training will have to be more intensive. For example, at Intel, new hires participate in a six-month orientation. Throughout that period, employees follow a set curriculum, attending classes and learning about the organizational culture of Intel. Designing effective and efficient training programs thus begins with the hiring process. However, regardless of the effectiveness of the hiring process, the need to indoctrinate new employees provides another significant reason for training. The objectives of an employee orientation program should, at a minimum, consist of:

1. Providing realistic information about the job and the organization (organizational policies, processes, culture, etc.).

2. Offering support and assurance to a new employee.

3. Identifying organizational stressors that a new employee is likely to encounter, and providing training for coping with those stressors.

4. Allowing ample time for questions.

Training Content (Product)

The Purposes of Training

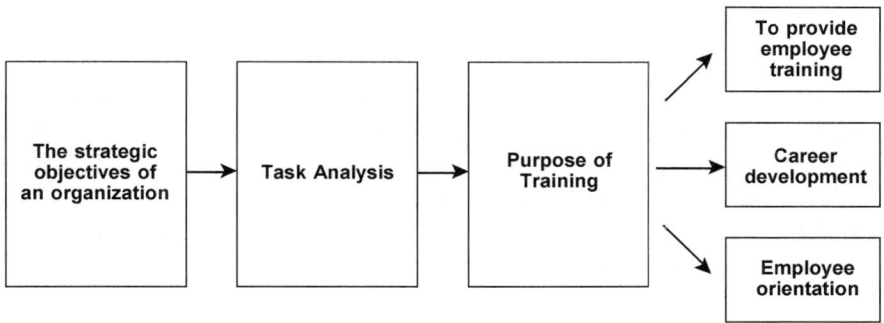

```
[The strategic objectives of an organization] → [Task Analysis] → [Purpose of Training] → [To provide employee training]
                                                                                         → [Career development]
                                                                                         → [Employee orientation]
```

Once the purpose of the training has been determined, you must confront the organizational constraints that limit training content. Type "A" or "B" cultures will usually impose fewer constraints than type "D" or "F" cultures. However, all organizations encounter scarcity and must face the reality that training will have to be limited.

Once you know the constraints associated with designing a training program, you can begin to develop the specific training content. As we explained in Chapter 4, learning is a relatively permanent change in human capabilities that is not a result of growth processes—capabilities related to specific learning outcomes (verbal information, intellectual skills, motor skills, attitudes, and cognitive strategies).

From that definition, use learning theory to develop training content, based on the purpose of the training and the organizational constraints that must be confronted.

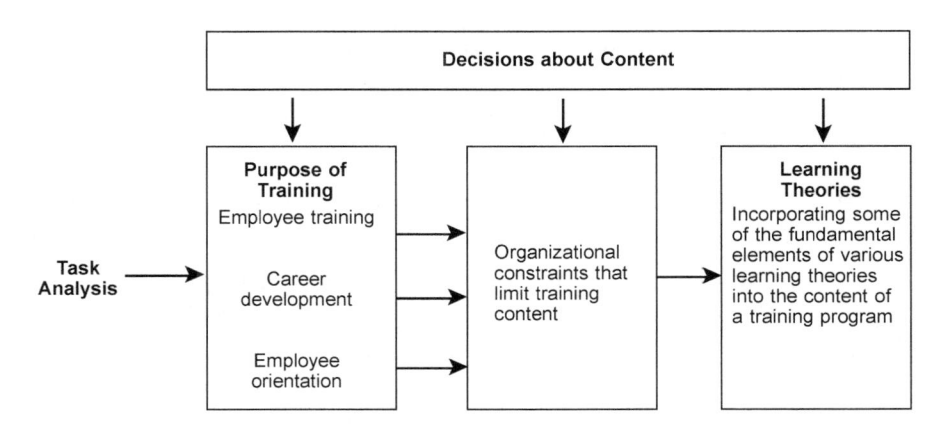

```
                    Decisions about Content
                    ↓              ↓              ↓
[Task Analysis] → Purpose of    Organizational   Learning
                  Training      constraints that Theories
                  Employee      limit training   Incorporating some
                  training      content          of the fundamental
                                                 elements of various
                  Career                         learning theories
                  development                    into the content of
                                                 a training program
                  Employee
                  orientation
```

83

The Impact of Learning Theories on the Training Process and Training Content

Each learning theory offers essential clues for designing an effective and efficient training experience. The great fictional detective Sherlock Holmes suggested that it's critically important to be able to recognize the vital clues from the incidental ones. What follows is a list of vital clues or facts that influence the training process and training content, as suggested by Hellriegel, Slocum, and Woodman; Gordon; Noe; and the author.

Training Tips

- What a trainee learns will be influenced by the response of a trainer to an action, behavior, or statement of a trainee. Punishments and rewards can play a critical role in determining what is learned. Reinforce proper actions, behaviors, and statements and discourage improper actions, behaviors, and statements.

- A trainee can learn by watching others who act as models. For the models to be effective, the desired behaviors, actions, or skills need to be clearly specified, and the model should have characteristics (such as age or position) similar to the target audience. After observing the model, trainees should have the opportunity to reproduce the skills and behaviors shown by the model.

- A trainer must keep the attention of a trainee focused on what is being modeled or studied, and must also understand how incentives and motivational processes can positively or negatively influence retention and repetition.

- Identify specific objectives or goals that should be achieved from the training. The training objective or goal should comprise three components:

  1. An explanation of what the employee is expected to do (performance).

  2. A statement of the quality or level of performance that is acceptable (criterion).

  3. A declaration of the conditions under which the trainee is expected to perform the desired outcome (conditions).

- A trainer should be aware of the needs of a trainee and should communicate how the training can fulfill those needs.
- Learning is most likely to occur when a trainee believes that his or her effort will lead to a particular outcome AND the outcome is valued by the trainee.
- A trainee tends to learn better when the training is linked to his or her current job experiences AND when the trainee has an opportunity to determine certain aspects or characteristics of the learning situation.
- A trainee learns best when he or she has the opportunity to practice what is being studied. The trainer should explain what trainees will be doing; the criteria for attainment of the objective; and the conditions under which the practice sessions will be conducted.
- Trainees need feedback that is focused on specific behaviors—and it must be provided immediately.
- Trainees need the training program to be properly coordinated and arranged. Good coordination ensures that trainees are not distracted by factors such as an uncomfortable room or poorly organized materials that could interfere with learning.
- To be effective and efficient, training should be linked with the strategic objectives of an organization.
- Each trainee should be treated in an objective, fair, and equitable manner.

The purpose of the training, the organizational constraints, and adult learning theory all must shape the content of a training program in much the same way as a sculptor molds clay into a work of art.

Strategic Training: Putting Employees First

Shaping Training Content

↑ ↑ ↑

The Vital Facts Regarding Learning Theories and Training

Learning Theory	Implications for the Training Process and Content
Reinforcement Theory	Reinforce proper actions, behaviors, and statements; discourage improper actions, behaviors, or statements.
Social Learning Theory	A trainee can learn by watching others (who act as models).
Social Learning Theory	A trainer must keep the attention of a trainee focused on what is being modeled or studied, and should understand how incentives and motivational processes can positively or negatively influence retention and reproduction.
Goal-Setting Theory	Identify specific objectives or goals that should be achieved from the training.
Need Theories	The training should address the needs of the trainee.
Expectancy Theory	Learning is most likely to occur when a trainee believes that his or her effort will lead to a particular outcome AND that outcome is valued by the trainee.
Adult Learning Theory	A trainee tends to learn better when the training is linked to current job experiences AND when the trainee has some input as to how the training will be conducted.
Adult Learning Theory	A trainee learns best when he or she can practice what is being modeled or studied.
Adult Learning Theory	Feedback should focus on specific behaviors and be provided immediately.
Adult Learning Theory	The training content should be prepared carefully.
High-Leverage Training	Training should be linked to the strategic objectives of an organization and to adult learning theory.
Equity Theory	The training environment should be fair and objective.

↑ ↑ ↑

Organizational Constraints

↑ ↑ ↑

Purpose of Training

Training Delivery

The final product objective of the STEM model is to select a training methodology. Options range from lecturing in a classroom setting, videos, or technology-based training (other than e-training or e-learning or a combination of options) to simulations, virtual reality, computer-assisted instruction (CAI), role play, mentoring, coaching, job rotation, peer training, case studies, team training, guest speakers, trainee presentations, apprenticeships, tuition assistance, games, adventure learning (wilderness or outdoor training), and e-training (e-learning).

Most of the presentation options listed above are self-explanatory, with the possible exceptions of adventure learning (wilderness or outdoor training) and e-training (e-learning). Adventure learning attempts to develop teamwork and leadership skills through structured outdoor activities. E-learning generally refers to the use of technology-based learning systems that involve a wide range of electronic media. In more-specific terms, e-training (e-learning) has been referred to as synchronous or asynchronous learning that is conducted over the Internet, intranet, extranet, or other Internet-based technology. *Synchronous* or *asynchronous* learning simply refers to the ability of a trainee (or learner) to work online with or without others. E-training (e-learning) includes computer-based training, Web-based training, distributed learning, virtual classroom, and distance learning. E-training (e-learning) activities include the following:

- **Computer-based training (CBT).** Computers are used to manage and present content to trainees. The learning process is self-paced and can be individualized. Most computer-based training is interactive, including simulations, problem solving, and games.

- **CD-ROM courses.** Courses are presented by means of read-only memory compact discs. Such courses have given way to Web-based training.

- **Web-based training (WBT).** Computers are used with Internet or corporate intranet access by means of a Web browser. A Web browser is a software program that can be used to conduct research, such as on the World Wide Web (www). WBT allows trainees to control the pace of learning.

- **Performance Support Systems (PSSs).** A combination of expert coaches and mentors, documents, and decision support tools are used to help a trainee make proper decisions on the job.

- **Electronic Performance Support Systems (EPSSs).** Similar to performance support systems, such systems use computers to store, capture, reconfigure, and distribute information to assist trainees.

- **Distance learning.** This instructional delivery technique does not require a trainee to be physically present in the same location as a trainer.

- **Distributed learning.** This type of learning is similar to distance learning, but training resources are distributed, thus allowing a trainee to have more control over his or her learning because they can access resource materials as needed.

- **Webinars.** Webinars are live training demonstrations and seminars that are delivered to a dispersed audience utilizing real-time audio and video.

Product Content Decisions and Delivery Options

Once you have made decisions about product content (purpose of training, organizational constraints, and the specific training content based on some of the fundamental elements of various learning theories), you are ready to consider training methods and techniques.

The table that follows presents a varied menu of such options.

Training Content (Product)

Workplace Training Methods and Techniques

Employee Training	Career Development	Employee Orientation
Lecturing	Videos	Lecturing
Videos	Tuition assistance	Videos
Technology-based training (simulations, virtual reality, or computer-assisted instruction)	Technology-based training (simulations, virtual reality, or computer-assisted instruction)	Technology-based training (simulations, virtual reality, or computer-assisted instruction)
Tuition assistance	Role play	Role play
Role play	Mentoring	Guest speakers
Mentoring	Coaching	Games
Coaching	Job rotation	
Job rotation	Peer training	
Peer training	Team training	
Case studies	Apprenticeships	
Team training	Games	
Trainee presentations	Adventure learning	
Apprenticeships	E-training (e-learning)	
E-training (e-learning)		
Adventure learning		

↑ ↑ ↑

Shaping Training Content

↑ ↑ ↑

Decisions around training content (purpose of training, organizational constraints, and the specific training content based on some of the fundamental elements of various learning theories)

Critical Points in Chapter 7

Critical Point 1

Product objectives at the micro-organizational training level of the STEM model consist of decisions about product content and delivery and presentation options.

Critical Point 2

Decisions must be made regarding the purpose of the training (employee training, career development, employee orientation); organizational constraints; and specific training content that will be based on some of the fundamental elements of learning theory.

Critical Point 3

Presentation options include lecturing in a classroom setting, videos, and technology-based training (other than e-training or e-learning), simulations, virtual reality, computer-assisted instruction (CAI), role play, mentoring, coaching, job rotation, peer training, case studies, team training, guest speakers, trainee presentations, apprenticeships, tuition assistance, games, adventure learning (wilderness or outdoor training), and e-training (e-learning).

Critical Point 4

Content decisions and delivery and presentation options shape the content of a training program.

Training Content (Product)

The Strategic Training of Employees Model (STEM) (after Including Product Objectives)

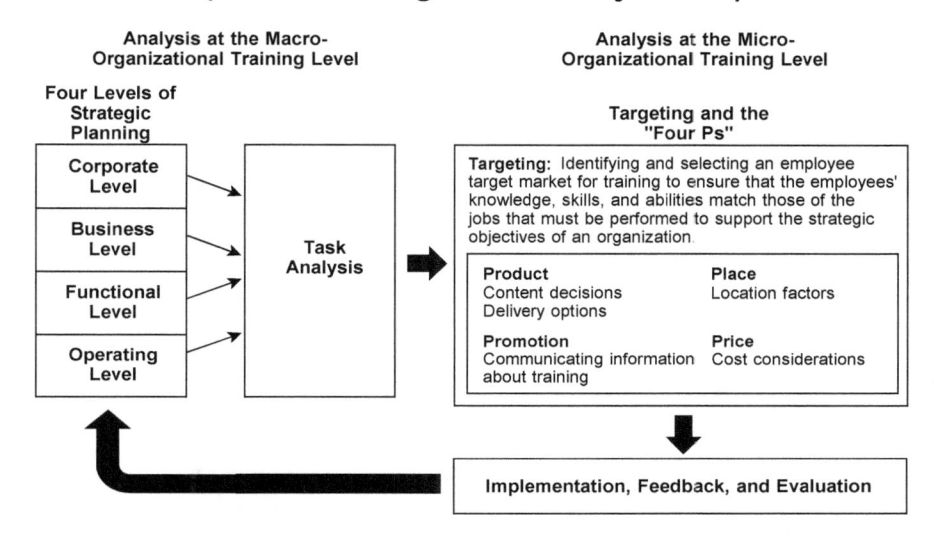

Analysis at the Macro-Organizational Training Level

Four Levels of Strategic Planning:
- Corporate Level
- Business Level
- Functional Level
- Operating Level

→ Task Analysis →

Analysis at the Micro-Organizational Training Level

Targeting and the "Four Ps"

Targeting: Identifying and selecting an employee target market for training to ensure that the employees' knowledge, skills, and abilities match those of the jobs that must be performed to support the strategic objectives of an organization.

Product Content decisions Delivery options	**Place** Location factors
Promotion Communicating information about training	**Price** Cost considerations

↓

Implementation, Feedback, and Evaluation

"Place" (distribution) is all about getting the right product to the right target market at the right location and time.

Chapter 8
Location Factors
(Place)

Logistics management is about delivering products to buyers when and where they want them, at a reasonable cost. The location or place objectives at the micro-organizational training level of our STEM model are similar to logistics in that the "place" function of the model has to do with delivering quality training programs to employee target markets effectively and efficiently.

> **Place Analysis**
>
> Place analysis focuses on:
> - On-the-job training (OJT)
> - Off-the-job training
> - Facility decisions
> - Equipment decisions
> - Decisions about supplies
> - Outsourcing of training

In OJT, the trainee works on-site, usually under the supervision of an experienced worker, supervisor, or trainer. Examples of OJT include job rotation, apprenticeships, and internships. Here are the basics:

Preparing for on-the-job instruction:

- Break down the job into critical steps.
- Prepare any necessary equipment, materials, and supplies.
- Determine how much time will be devoted to OJT. There should be enough time for most trainees to acquire the necessary skills to perform the job.

Actual instruction:

- Explain to the trainee the objectives of the task, and ask the trainee to watch you demonstrate it.
- Perform the task without speaking.
- After demonstrating, explain and write out the key points, steps, or behaviors.
- Demonstrate the task again.
- Have the trainee perform at least part of the job task, and praise the trainee when he or she does it correctly.
- Have the trainee perform the entire job task, and praise him or her when it is done correctly.
- If mistakes are made, have the trainee practice until the task is performed correctly.
- Praise the trainee for his or her success in learning the job task.

Off-the-job training is an alternative to OJT. Common examples are formal courses, simulations, and role-playing exercises in a classroom setting. Some of the decisions that must be made for classroom environments have to do with noise level, colors, room structure, lighting, wall and floor coverings, type of chairs, ceiling height, electrical outlets, acoustics, and the glare from metal surfaces, TV monitors, or mirrors. The seating arrangement should also be considered; seating formats range from a fan-type setting, classroom-type setting, conference-type setting, and horseshoe arrangements.

Decisions regarding equipment will naturally focus on media learning tools such as audiovisual- or computer-based equipment and possibly "intelligent" tutoring or expert systems equipment (e-training or e-learning systems).

Supplies that might be needed include: handouts, paper, pens, pencils, markers, textbooks, chalkboards or whiteboards, chart paper and easels, and other learning materials.

The best training location is a place that is comfortable, accessible, quiet, private, and free from interruptions, with enough space, equipment, and supplies to create a quality training environment.

Location Factors (Place)

Training Room Considerations

Training Room Conditions

Noise: Check for noise from heating/air conditioning systems, adjacent rooms or corridors, and sources outside the building.

Colors: Pastels tend to be warm colors. White and beige are cold and sterile, while blacks and browns appear to "close up" the room and can become fatiguing.

Room structure: Long and narrow rooms make it difficult to see and hear. Try to select a somewhat square room.

Lighting: Fluorescent lights should be the main source of lighting, but incandescent lighting should be spread throughout the room and controlled with a dimmer switch when projection is required.

Wall and floor coverings: Solid-color carpeting should be placed in the meeting area. Only training-related material should be on the walls.

Meeting room chairs: Chairs should be comfortable, with backs that support the lower lumbar region. Chairs with wheels that swivel are preferred.

Ceiling: Higher ceilings are preferred to lower ceilings (10-foot ceilings are recommended).

Electrical outlets: Ample electrical outlets and telephone jacks should be placed throughout the training room.

Acoustics: Check and monitor voice clarity and level throughout the training room.

Glare: Eliminate glare from metal surfaces, TV monitors, and mirrors.

Seating Arrangements

→ Fan-type seating allows trainees to easily switch from listening to a presentation to participating in discussions or practice learning activities.

This seating arrangement can also be used for group or team learning activities.

→ A classroom-type setting should be used for lecture and audio-visual presentations when the purpose of the training is primarily knowledge acquisition.

A conference-type setting encourages group discussion.

→ A horseshoe arrangement is desirable when group discussions and presentations will be part of the training experience.

Decisions regarding OJT, off-the-job training, facilities, equipment, and supplies are not the only location decisions that must be made. You will have to decide whether or not any of the training functions should be outsourced. If a particular training activity can be provided by an outside vendor at a lower cost (while ensuring quality), it should be subcontracted—as long as you know the training will be of high quality.

As reported in ASTD's 2004 State of the Industry Annual Review, the percentage of expenditures for external training services has risen steadily since 2002. The most-used sources of external training in 2003 were independent consultants (78%), universities (72%), and consulting firms (68%). The use of community colleges fell from 67% to 62% between 2002 and 2003, but reliance on vocational and technical institutions went from 48% to 54%. The least-used sources of external training in 2003 were unions and trade professionals (34%) and local, state, and federal governments (25%).

Location Factors (Place)

Critical Points in Chapter 8

Critical Point 1

"Place" analysis refers to decisions having to do with training location: on-the-job or off-the-job training, as well as criteria for facilities, equipment, and supplies. Decisions will also have to be made as to whether or not training should be provided by an outside source.

Critical Point 2

"Facility" considerations have to do with the training room and seating arrangements.

The Strategic Training of Employees Model (STEM)
(after Including Place Objectives)

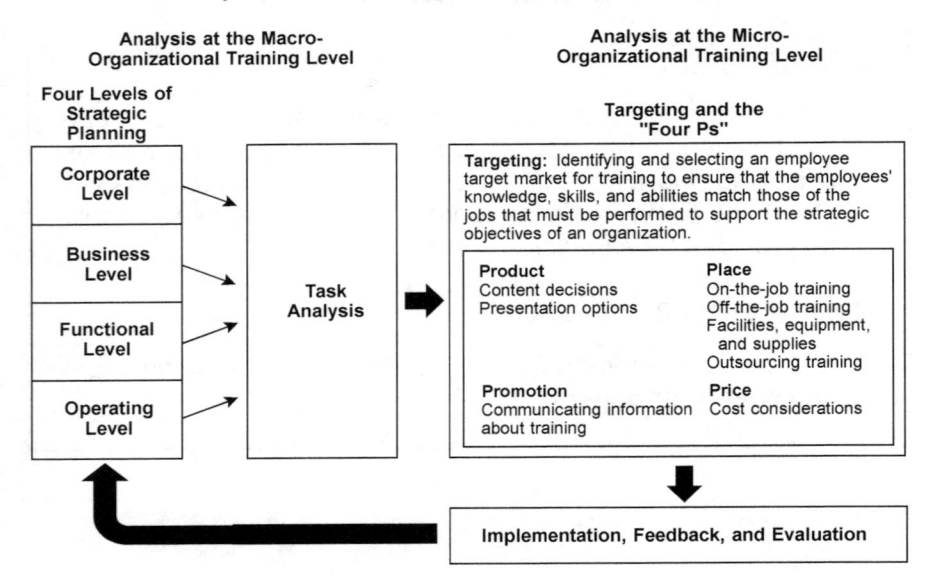

Analysis at the Macro-Organizational Training Level

Four Levels of Strategic Planning:
- Corporate Level
- Business Level
- Functional Level
- Operating Level

→ Task Analysis →

Analysis at the Micro-Organizational Training Level

Targeting and the "Four Ps"

Targeting: Identifying and selecting an employee target market for training to ensure that the employees' knowledge, skills, and abilities match those of the jobs that must be performed to support the strategic objectives of an organization.

Product
Content decisions
Presentation options

Place
On-the-job training
Off-the-job training
Facilities, equipment, and supplies
Outsourcing training

Promotion
Communicating information about training

Price
Cost considerations

↓

Implementation, Feedback, and Evaluation

> Promotion is all about getting the word out about the value of training.

Chapter 9
Communicating Information about Training Programs (Promotion)

From a strict marketing perspective, the purpose of promotion is to persuade a target market to purchase a product by informing them of the benefits of that product, and to remind current consumers why they should continue to buy the product.

Training promotion is about communicating factual information and persuasive messages about training issues and activities to prospective departments, units, and employee target markets within an organization. Effective informational or persuasive messages grab attention, instill interest, arouse desire, and induce a specific outcome. The ultimate promotion goal should be to create a permanent bond of trust between the training department and the other departments within the organization. Building trust will foster organizational support for the training function. In the end, that support will enlarge the role and the prestige of the training function. The actual level of managerial support for training can range from low support (which means that managers generally accept training and allow employees to attend training) to high support (where a manager actually helps with the training).

The most effective way to promote the training function is to get the HR department to become more strategic in scope and improve its overall image. Besides becoming involved in the strategic planning process, trainers should use the company newsletter to report training issues and events, and schedule ongoing visits between training department administrators and the managers of other departments to promote the benefits of training. The best form of promotion, however, is positive word-of-mouth communication among employees—and you only get that if you provide a quality training experience.

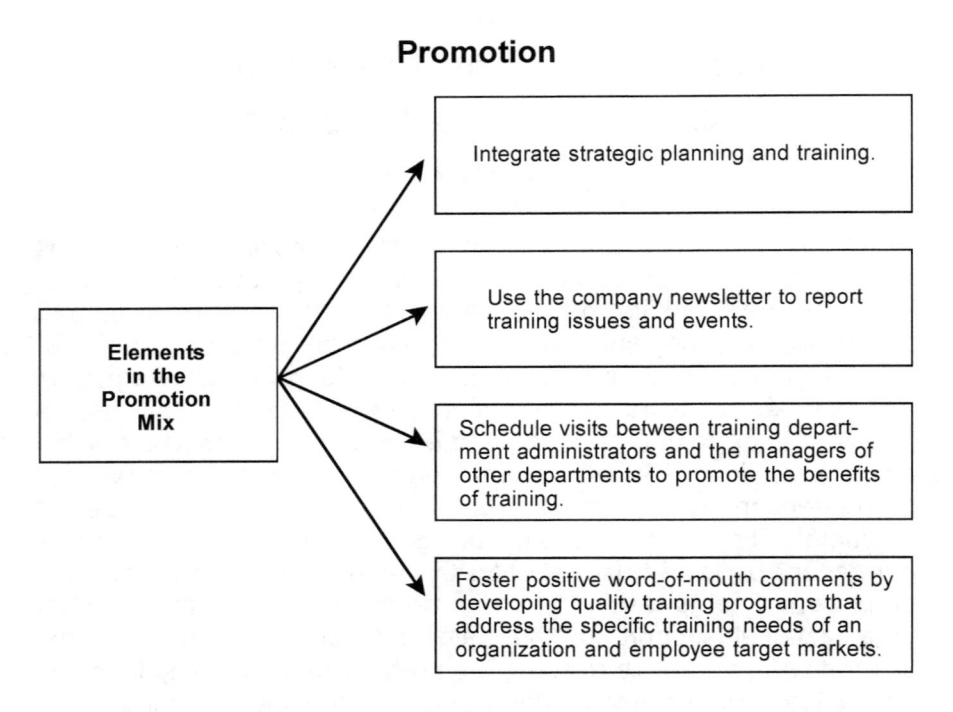

Strategic Training: Putting Employees First

Promotion

Elements in the Promotion Mix

- Integrate strategic planning and training.
- Use the company newsletter to report training issues and events.
- Schedule visits between training department administrators and the managers of other departments to promote the benefits of training.
- Foster positive word-of-mouth comments by developing quality training programs that address the specific training needs of an organization and employee target markets.

All the elements of the training promotion mix should be systematically coordinated so that you have an integrated training message that enhances the image of the training function among all internal stakeholders, ranging from senior management to clerical and maintenance personnel. You can raise the profile of the training function by making sure each manager is aware of all the training options, and then moving them along to knowledge, to liking, to stating preferences, to conviction, and to consistent use of various training programs, as can be seen in the representation that follows.

Communicating Information about Training Programs (Promotion)

The Training Hierarchy of Communication Effects

A consistent user of training programs
↑
Conviction (a supporter of training)
↑
A preference for training
↑
A liking of training
↑
Knowledge of training
↑
Awareness of training
↑
Complete lack of information regarding training options

Critical Points in Chapter 9

Critical Point 1

Training promotion in the STEM model is about communicating factual information and persuasive messages about training issues and activities to prospective departments, units, and employee target markets within the organization.

Critical Point 2

Training promotion consists of integrating strategic planning and training; using the company newsletter to report training issues and events; scheduling ongoing meetings between training department administrators and managers of other departments to promote the benefits of training; and fostering positive word-of-mouth communication.

Critical Point 3

The ultimate objective of the training promotion element of the STEM model is to develop a bond of trust between the training staff and staff members in other departments within an organization in order to gain support and increase the prestige of the training function.

Critical Point 4

Increasing the importance of the training function can be accomplished by moving internal stakeholders along a training hierarchy of effects and progressively raising awareness of its importance.

Critical Point 5

To promote the training, you must make every manager aware of the training and get them to progressively like it, prefer it, believe in it, and consistently use various training programs ("the training hierarchy of effects").

The Strategic Training of Employees Model (STEM)
(after Including Place Objectives)

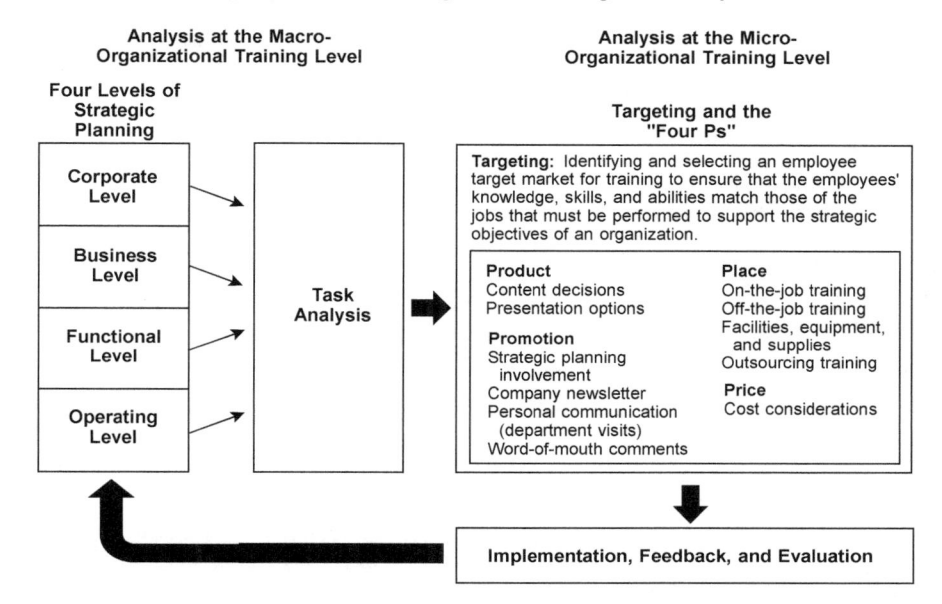

Analysis at the Macro-Organizational Training Level

Four Levels of Strategic Planning:
- Corporate Level
- Business Level
- Functional Level
- Operating Level

→ Task Analysis →

Analysis at the Micro-Organizational Training Level

Targeting and the "Four Ps"

Targeting: Identifying and selecting an employee target market for training to ensure that the employees' knowledge, skills, and abilities match those of the jobs that must be performed to support the strategic objectives of an organization.

Product
- Content decisions
- Presentation options

Promotion
- Strategic planning involvement
- Company newsletter
- Personal communication (department visits)
- Word-of-mouth comments

Place
- On-the-job training
- Off-the-job training
- Facilities, equipment, and supplies
- Outsourcing training

Price
- Cost considerations

↓

Implementation, Feedback, and Evaluation

> Paying attention to cost details related to a training program can make the difference between success and failure.

Chapter 10
Cost Considerations (Price)

The primary objective of a cost-accounting system is to gather cost information about the training product, such as costs related to materials, direct labor, and overhead. *Direct materials* costs have to do with the cost of the materials used in producing a product; *direct labor* refers to the wages of the employees that are directly involved in converting materials into a finished product; and *overhead* costs are costs other than direct materials or direct labor.

> **Product Costs (Price)**
>
> - Direct materials
> - Direct labor
> - Overhead costs

From a training perspective, cost or price analysis begins with identification of the specific costs associated with developing a training activity or program. There are traditionally seven cost sources, as articulated by R. Noe in 1999: (1) program development or purchase, (2) instructional materials, (3) equipment and hardware, (4) facilities, (5) travel and lodging, (6) salaries of trainers and support staff, and (7) loss of productivity while trainees attend the program (or the cost of hiring temporary employees who replace the trainees while they are at training) and trainees' salaries and benefits, based on time away from the job.

Strategic Training: Putting Employees First

```
┌─────────────────────────────────────────────┐
│      Cost Sources Associated with Training  │
└─────────────────────────────────────────────┘
         ↓              ↓              ↓
┌──────────────┐ ┌──────────────┐ ┌──────────────┐
│Direct Materials│ │ Direct Labor │ │Overhead Costs│
└──────────────┘ └──────────────┘ └──────────────┘
                        ↓
          Program Development or Purchase
                        ↓
                Instructional Materials
                        ↓
                Equipment and Hardware
                        ↓
                      Facilities
                        ↓
                 Travel and Lodging
                        ↓
           Salaries of Trainers and Support Staff
                        ↓
                    Trainee Costs
```

Loss of productivity while trainees attend the program (or the cost of hiring temporary employees to replace the trainees while they are at training) and trainees' salaries and benefits, based on time away from the job.

Use the cost sources associated with training and modify the standard definitions of direct materials, direct labor, and overhead costs to determine specific training costs.

Cost Considerations (Price)

Costs Associated with Developing an In-House Training Program

Direct Materials	Direct Labor	Overhead
Definition associated with training	Definition associated with training	Definition associated with training
The cost of the materials directly used in producing a training program	The salaries/wages and fringe benefits that are directly involved in developing a training program	All other training costs that are used to develop a training program (other than direct materials or direct labor)
Instructional materials expenses	Trainer salaries/wages and fringe benefits (25% to 35% of salary) directly associated with developing a training program	**Trainee Costs** Trainees' wages/salaries and fringe benefits (based on time away from their job)
Miscellaneous supplies expenses (supplies used in developing a training program, other than instructional materials)	Other training department salaries/wages and fringe benefits (clerical or administrative) directly associated with developing a training program	Loss of productivity while trainees attend the program (or cost of hiring temporary workers to replace the trainees while they attend the training session)
Postage, shipping	Clerical and administrative support (salaries/wages and fringe benefits directly associated with developing a training program)	Equipment and hardware expenses
	External consulting expenses	Refreshments
		Facilities expenses (classroom space and utilities)
		Travel and lodging expenses
		Overhead supplies (other than direct supplies)

The chart that follows outlines the various costs associated with a training program that is purchased from an outside source.

Strategic Training: Putting Employees First

Costs Associated with Purchasing a Training Program		
Direct Materials	**Direct Labor**	**Overhead**
Definition associated with training	Definition associated with training	Definition associated with training
The cost of the materials directly associated with purchase of the training program and/or the learning itself	The salaries/wages and fringe benefits directly associated with purchasing the training program and/or the learning itself	All other training costs associated with the purchase of the training program and/or the learning itself (other than direct materials or direct labor)
Instructional materials expenses	Trainer salaries/wages and fringe benefits (25% to 35% of salary) directly associated with purchasing the training program and/or the learning itself	Cost of the training program and registration fees
Miscellaneous supplies expenses	Other training department salaries/wages and fringe benefits (clerical or administrative) associated with purchasing the training program and/or the learning itself	**Trainee Costs**
		Trainees' wages/salaries and fringe benefits (based on time away from their job)
Postage, shipping	Clerical and administrative support (salaries/wages and fringe benefits associated with purchasing the training program and/or the learning itself)	Loss of productivity while trainees attend the program (or cost of hiring temporary workers to replace the trainees while they attend the training session)
		Refreshments
		Facilities expenses (classroom space and utilities)
		Travel and lodging expenses
		Overhead supplies (other than direct supplies)
		Equipment and hardware expenses

Cost Considerations (Price)

There will be many costs associated with a training program, whether it is developed in-house or purchased from an outside source. Develop an aggregate annual training budget by first identifying the costs per session, and then multiplying the total cost of each training session by the number of training sessions forecasted for the year. Do this for each program you are sponsoring.

For example, suppose that your organization is rather small and will be offering the following training sessions:

- 3 training sessions, with a total estimated cost of $1,500 per session

- 10 training sessions, with a total estimated cost of $800 per session

- 1 training session, with a total estimated cost of $13,000

Your aggregate annual training budget would be 3($1,500) + 10($800) + 1($13,000) or $4,500 + $8,000 + $13,000 or $25,500.

We'll take a closer look at cost considerations and all the other critical areas related to training later. In the next chapter, we focus on implementation.

Critical Points in Chapter 10

Critical Point 1

The costs associated with training include the costs of: (1) program development or purchase, (2) instructional materials, (3) equipment and hardware, (4) facilities, (5) travel and lodging, (6) salaries of trainers and support staff, and (7) loss of productivity while trainees attend the program (or the cost of hiring temporary employees to replace the trainees while they are at training) and trainees' salaries and benefits (based on time away from the job).

Critical Point 2

Use the cost sources associated with training and modify the standard definitions of direct materials, direct labor, and overhead costs to determine specific training costs for each training program.

Critical Point 3

Develop an aggregate annual training budget by first identifying the costs for each training program, and then multiplying the total cost of each training program by the number of training sessions forecasted for the year.

Cost Considerations (Price)

The Strategic Training of Employees Model (STEM)
(after Including Price Objectives)

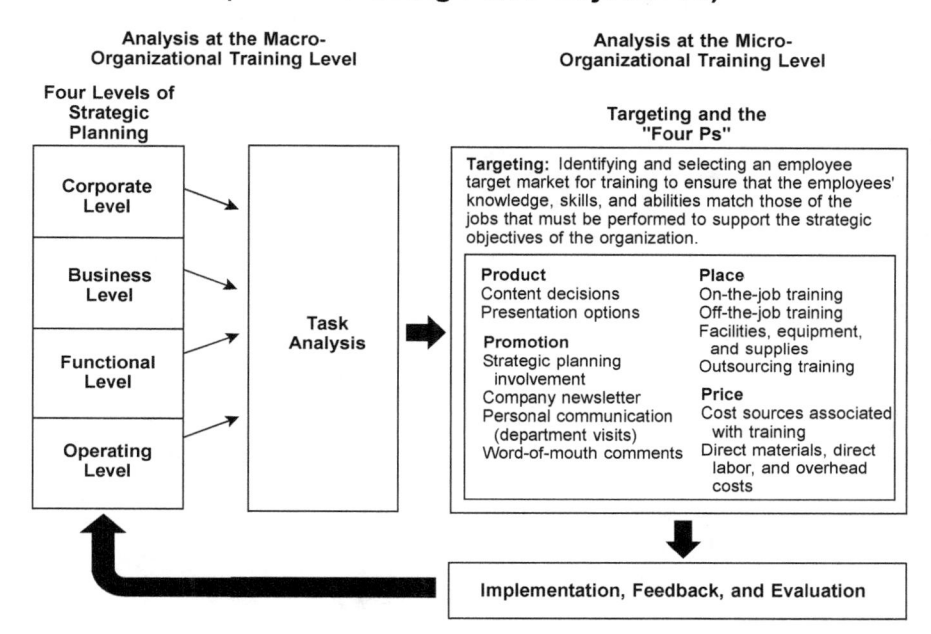

Analysis at the Macro-Organizational Training Level

Four Levels of Strategic Planning:
- Corporate Level
- Business Level
- Functional Level
- Operating Level

→ Task Analysis →

Analysis at the Micro-Organizational Training Level

Targeting and the "Four Ps"

Targeting: Identifying and selecting an employee target market for training to ensure that the employees' knowledge, skills, and abilities match those of the jobs that must be performed to support the strategic objectives of the organization.

Product
Content decisions
Presentation options

Promotion
Strategic planning involvement
Company newsletter
Personal communication (department visits)
Word-of-mouth comments

Place
On-the-job training
Off-the-job training
Facilities, equipment, and supplies
Outsourcing training

Price
Cost sources associated with training
Direct materials, direct labor, and overhead costs

↓

Implementation, Feedback, and Evaluation

117

> Feedback provides a check against misunderstandings.
>
> – Stephen Robbins

Chapter 11
Implementation, Feedback, and Evaluation

After a training program has been developed, the next phase in our organizational training analysis is to implement the program. Feedback is an important part of implementation; in fact, you must have an ongoing evaluation process in place to ensure that the quality of the training does not diminish.

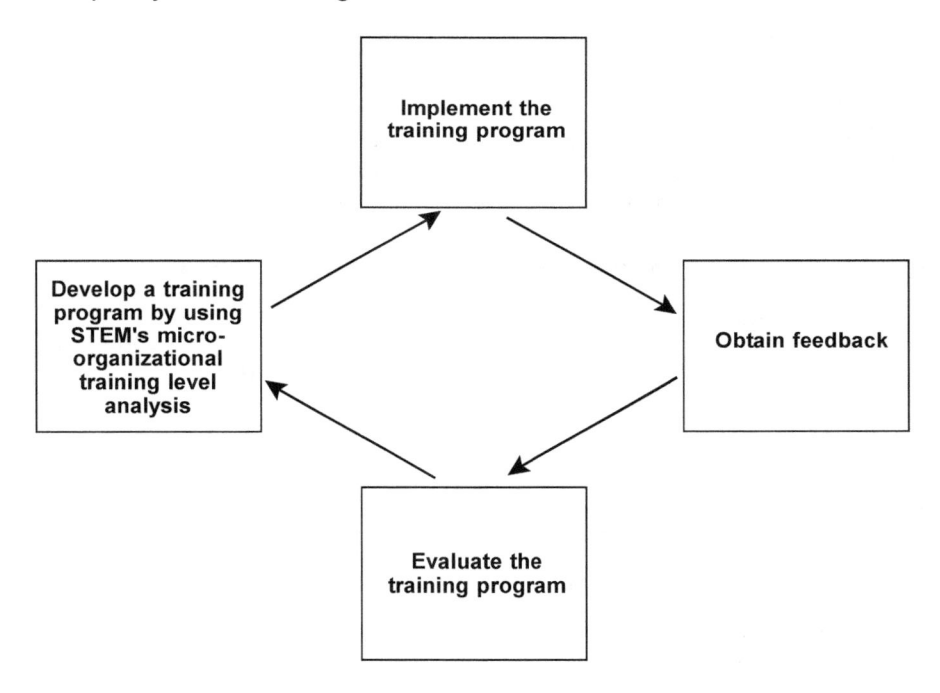

```
           Implement the
          training program
         ↗              ↘
Develop a training           Obtain feedback
program by using
STEM's micro-
organizational
training level
analysis
         ↖              ↙
           Evaluate the
          training program
```

Communication is a critical determinant in the success of the implementation, feedback, and evaluation phase of the training model.

Stages in the Communication Process

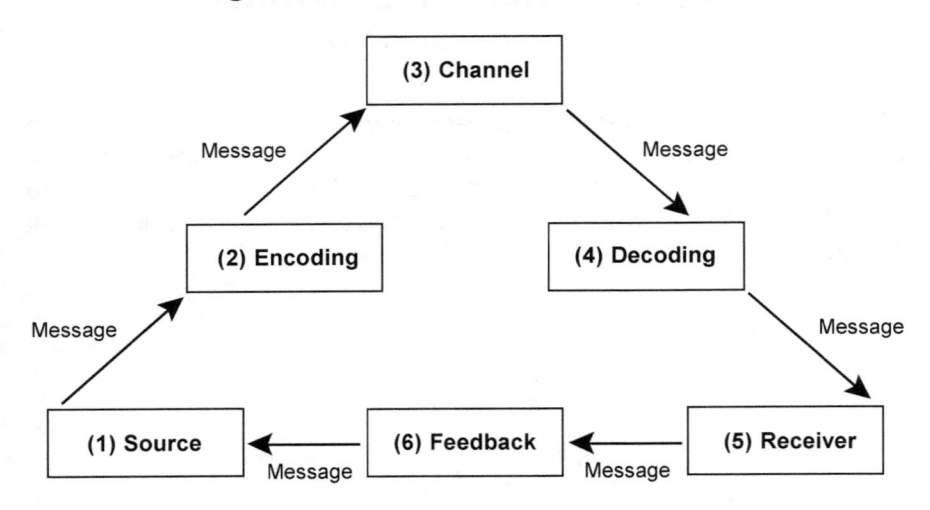

```
                    ┌─────────────┐
                    │ (3) Channel │
                    └─────────────┘
                   ↗               ↘
           Message                   Message
         ┌──────────────┐       ┌──────────────┐
         │ (2) Encoding │       │ (4) Decoding │
         └──────────────┘       └──────────────┘
        ↗                                       ↘
  Message                                         Message
┌────────────┐   ┌──────────────┐   ┌──────────────┐
│ (1) Source │ ← │ (6) Feedback │ ← │ (5) Receiver │
└────────────┘   └──────────────┘   └──────────────┘
              Message           Message
```

Source of a message: The originator or sender of the message

Encoding: The process by which the sender of a message translates the idea to be communicated into a symbolic message that consists of words, pictures, numbers, and gestures

Message: What is being communicated

Channel: The medium through which a message is communicated to a receiver

Decoding: The retranslation of a message by the receiver

Receiver: The one to whom the message is directed

Feedback: The communication of the receiver's reaction to the message

Communication between a sender and a receiver is perfect when the encoded message is exactly the same as the decoded message. Any breakdowns or interference in the communication process will result in inaccurate information being transmitted. Communication experts refer to a disruption or distraction in the communication process as *noise*. Noise can cause miscommunication and inaccurate communication of information, which can limit the effectiveness of implementation, feedback, and evaluation.

Implementation, Feedback, and Evaluation

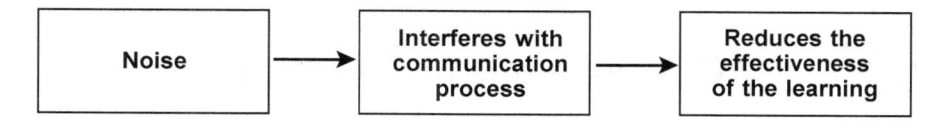

```
┌─────────┐     ┌──────────────┐     ┌──────────────┐
│         │     │ Interferes with│     │ Reduces the  │
│  Noise  │ ──▶ │ communication │ ──▶ │ effectiveness│
│         │     │   process     │     │ of the learning│
└─────────┘     └──────────────┘     └──────────────┘
```

Training professionals should do their best to avoid sending conflicting messages or using terminology that might be misunderstood, because while they are not generally thought of as noise, they do interfere with the message. Limiting these kinds of interference, including distracting background sounds, makes it less likely that you will get accurate and reliable feedback, which you must have if you are to effectively evaluate the quality of your training program.

If you know you have obtained accurate feedback, try to identify the benefits of the training that was provided. You can use any of several techniques. Compare the feedback information to the benefits that have already been cited in the technical, academic, or practitioner literature and conduct pilot training programs to assess the value of the training. Observe the on-the-job performance of the employees after they have received the training. These are good assessment tools.

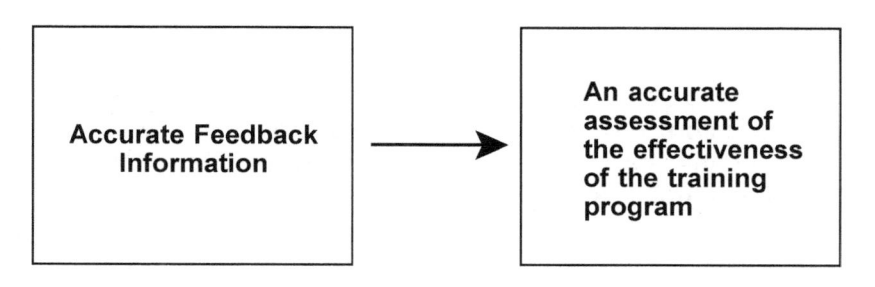

```
┌──────────────────────┐         ┌──────────────────────┐
│                      │         │   An accurate        │
│  Accurate Feedback   │   ──▶   │   assessment of      │
│     Information      │         │   the effectiveness  │
│                      │         │   of the training    │
│                      │         │   program            │
└──────────────────────┘         └──────────────────────┘
```

Strategic Training: Putting Employees First

Critical Points in Chapter 11

Critical Point 1

Communication is a critical determinant of the success of the implementation, feedback, and evaluation phase of the strategic training model.

Critical Point 2

The communication process consists of six stages: the source of the message, encoding the message, the channel or medium of transmission, decoding, receiving, and feedback.

Critical Point 3

"Noise" disrupts the communication process. Training professionals must do their best to reduce the sources of noise and anything else that is distracting.

Critical Point 4

Once the noise level has been reduced and accurate feedback information has been obtained, use any of a number of techniques to obtain accurate feedback regarding the training that was provided.

Implementation, Feedback, and Evaluation

The Strategic Training of Employees Model (STEM) (after Including Implementation, Feedback, and Evaluation)

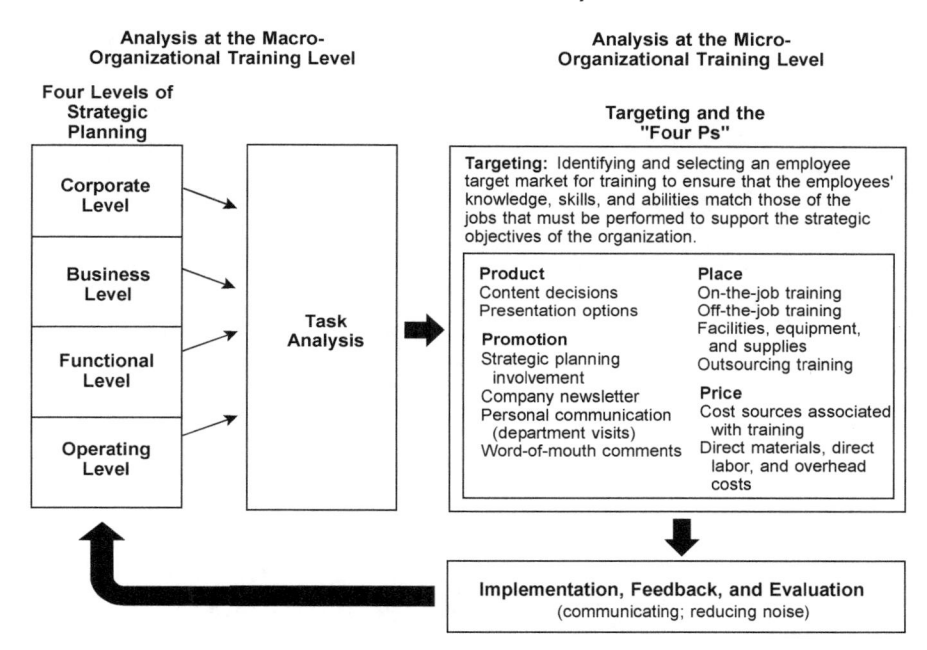

Analysis at the Macro-Organizational Training Level

Four Levels of Strategic Planning

- Corporate Level
- Business Level
- Functional Level
- Operating Level

→ Task Analysis →

Analysis at the Micro-Organizational Training Level

Targeting and the "Four Ps"

Targeting: Identifying and selecting an employee target market for training to ensure that the employees' knowledge, skills, and abilities match those of the jobs that must be performed to support the strategic objectives of the organization.

Product
Content decisions
Presentation options

Promotion
Strategic planning involvement
Company newsletter
Personal communication (department visits)
Word-of-mouth comments

Place
On-the-job training
Off-the-job training
Facilities, equipment, and supplies
Outsourcing training

Price
Cost sources associated with training
Direct materials, direct labor, and overhead costs

↓

Implementation, Feedback, and Evaluation
(communicating; reducing noise)

125

Part III:
Completing the Picture

> All models simplify reality in order to improve our understanding of it.
>
> – Gregory Mankiw

Chapter 12
How the STEM Model Can Help Organizations Solve Training Problems

We have completed our presentation of the Strategic Training of Employees Model (STEM). Let's now pause to consider the purpose of a model. As you know, a model captures the important elements of a problem that's being studied. It does not have to spell out every detail and interrelationship. In fact, the more details a model contains, the more unwieldy and less useful it becomes. The STEM model gives us a new way of increasing the value of the product or service that an organization brings to the marketplace.

Employee performance is primarily influenced by an organization's hiring and training practices. A thorough process that seeks out individuals who have a good work ethic and a successful educational and/or technical background, coupled with a quality training environment, can create the conditions under which employee productivity and organizational success will thrive. Organizations that eliminate training programs to cut costs essentially shoot themselves in the foot.

A thorough hiring process and a quality training environment	=	Quality employees at all levels within an organization	=	Organizational Success

Today's organizations face an assortment of training problems. I recently asked two colleagues to list the 15 most-important training problems or challenges facing 21st century organizations. Dr. Glen Boyce, vice president for community and workforce development at Holmes Community College, and Michael Blankenship, workforce development coordinator at Holmes, have worked with such organizations as American Packaging, BankPlus, Delphi, Eaton Aerospace, Environmental Solutions, Haverty Furniture Company, Levi Strauss, Milwaukee Electric Tool Corporation, Nissan North America, Nationwide Insurance, Siemens, University Medical Center, and Weyerhauser. The list that follows comes from their combined experience.

The 15 Most Important Training and Development Problems Facing Organizations

1. Inadequate social skills (insufficient ability to communicate and relate with other employees)

2. Poor work ethic (insufficient sense of urgency to accomplish tasks within the organized structure; not arriving to work on time)

3. Inadequate language skills (insufficient reading, writing, or speaking skills)

4. Inadequate communication skills (little or no ability to listen and interpret the message correctly and relate the message accurately to others)

5. Inadequate problem-solving skills (insufficient ability to interpret and infer meaning from data and draw logical conclusions)

6. Inadequate technical skills (insufficient skills necessary to operate in today's manufacturing or office environment)

7. Poor math skills (little or no ability to perform and understand mathematical calculations)

8. Imbalance of production time versus training time (While it is important to train in order to continue to be profitable, some companies reduce training in order to focus on production. There must be a balance of the two.)

9. No strategic approach to training

10. Poor hiring practices

11. Little or no understanding of the type of training that is needed (no needs analysis)

12. Inadequate training resources and no sense of where to go for resources, assistance, and training expertise

13. Little or no management training

14. Inadequate skill sets

15. No positive environment where employees want to excel and are motivated to learn and develop their skills and abilities

How the STEM Model Can Help Organizations

The STEM model can help address these training problems. It is based on the premise that all training should flow from the strategic objectives of an organization. Begin by asking this question:

> Does the training problem have strategic significance for the organization?

If not, then no training should be provided for that training problem. If the training problem has strategic ramifications for the organization, use the four Ps (product content, place, price, and promotion) to gather information on training options. Then identify the most appropriate training solution.

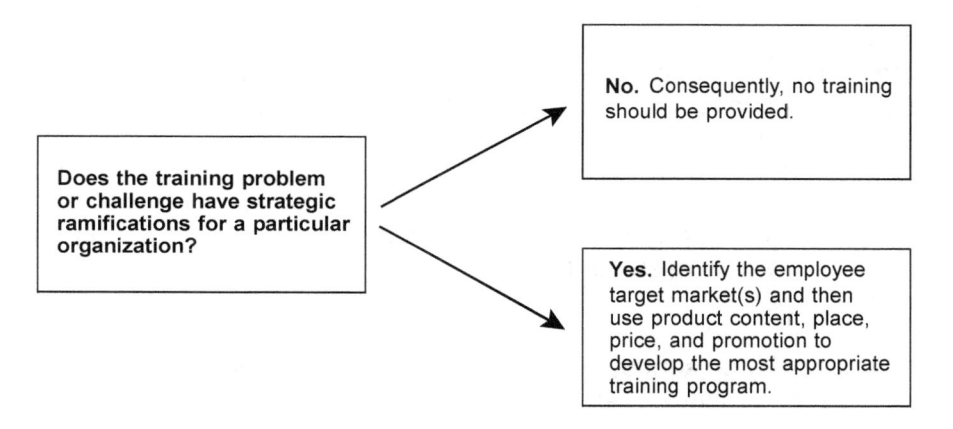

```
                                    ┌─────────────────────────────┐
                                    │ No. Consequently, no training│
                                ┌──▶│ should be provided.          │
                                │   └─────────────────────────────┘
┌──────────────────────────┐────┤
│ Does the training problem│    │
│ or challenge have strategic│   │
│ ramifications for a particular│ │   ┌─────────────────────────────┐
│ organization?            │    │   │ Yes. Identify the employee   │
└──────────────────────────┘────┤   │ target market(s) and then    │
                                └──▶│ use product content, place,  │
                                    │ price, and promotion to      │
                                    │ develop the most appropriate │
                                    │ training program.            │
                                    └─────────────────────────────┘
```

How can the STEM model help an organization address its most important training and development needs?

In this section, we will demonstrate how to use the STEM model to address important training and development needs.

Social skills (ability to communicate with others). Ask yourself if improving employees' social skills is a strategic objective for your organization. If it is not, then do not provide training in this area. Social skills might not be that significant in an industry in which the bulk of the tasks performed are highly structured or when the tasks being performed are primarily conducted in an isolated setting (such as intense truck driving or the duties of a night watchman).

If social skills are important, identify the target markets for training. When you have enough information on product content, place, price, and promotion, you might conclude that the most appropriate training solution is to develop an in-house, off-the-job training program conducted in a classroom setting, utilizing lecturing, role playing, and case studies. Another organization might decide that a less-formal training session augmented with mentoring and coaching can address this training need. A third organization might come to the conclusion that it is better to enroll employees in communication courses at a community college or four-year educational institution.

The strength of the STEM model is that it provides a comprehensive framework to analyze specific training situations and requirements, yet is flexible enough to give organizational decision makers a wide range of solutions. The training solution should only be selected after you have considered all factors, compared the cost of in-house training with what it will cost to outsource your training, and identified which solution is the best match for the organization.

Let's see how the model can be used to address other specific needs. We will assume that these needs have strategic significance.

Work Ethic (a sense of urgency to accomplish tasks within the organized structure). An organization might decide that it is too expensive to develop an in-house training program, in which case it can purchase a training program and use a Web-based, e-training delivery system to maximize employee exposure (while minimizing delivery costs). Another organization might decide to use adventure learning that stresses the importance of accomplishing tasks in a specific time frame to achieve group success. A third organization might prefer to develop its own on-the-job training program, focusing on employee productivity by helping employees achieve output standards.

Language Skills (reading, writing, and speaking skills). After product content, place, price, and promotion information has been reviewed, decision makers might conclude that the most appropriate training methodology will be to provide tuition assistance to employees who take classes in reading, writing, or public speaking at a community college or four-year academic institution. An in-house training program using an e-training delivery method or a self-paced training program (where employees are given time off from their job to review the program) are other options.

Communication Skills (listening and interpreting the message, and relating the message to others). Adventure learning can help employees improve their two-way communication skills. Formal classroom training that incorporates role-play activities and videos is also a good way to improve communication skills.

Problem-solving Skills (being able to interpret and infer meaning from data). Mentoring or coaching might be the training technique for a particular organization, whereby inexperienced employees are teamed up with experienced mentors or coaches who guide them through the various steps necessary to solve complex problems. Another organization might determine that so-called business games are the best way to build enthusiasm for problem solving.

Technical Skills (those skills necessary to operate in today's manufacturing or office environment). Many organizations address the need for improved technical skills by offering apprenticeships, job rotations, peer training, or adventure learning experiences. There are other effective options, such as sending employees to a technical training program offered at a community college or four-year educational institution, or even working directly with an academic institution to establish organizational-specific technical training programs.

Math Skills (the ability to perform and understand mathematical calculations). Once the information in the STEM model has been reviewed, an organization might conclude that the best way to train for math skills is to provide tuition assistance so that employees can take math courses at a community college or four-year academic institution, but another option is to purchase computer software that employees can use at work to improve their mathematical skills and abilities.

The Need to Balance Production Time and Training Time. Taking time to train without falling behind on production is a common organizational challenge. Training must be practical! No organization has unlimited resources. If you follow the STEM model and directly link training to your organization's strategic objectives, already-limited resources can be allocated effectively and efficiently. A training model must account for scarcity and limited resources, or it is worthless.

A Strategic Approach to Training. The STEM model is all about linking organizational strategy with training, as we see in this next illustration:

Strategic Planning is the Starting Point of the Model

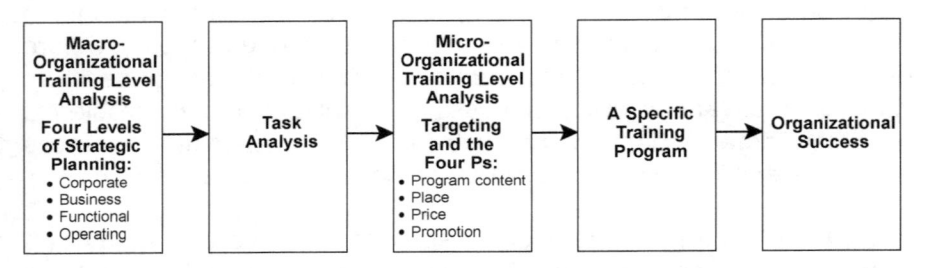

| Macro-Organizational Training Level Analysis

Four Levels of Strategic Planning:
• Corporate
• Business
• Functional
• Operating | → | Task Analysis | → | Micro-Organizational Training Level Analysis

Targeting and the Four Ps:
• Program content
• Place
• Price
• Promotion | → | A Specific Training Program | → | Organizational Success |

The organization must make sure that its strategic plans are directly linked with training. Consequently, its director of training must play an integral part in the strategic planning process.

Good Hiring Practices. We have already said that the hiring and training process of an organization dramatically impacts the quality of the employees, and that putting employees first should be a top priority. Your present employees suffer the effects of bad hires, which is one more reason to focus on improving hiring practices.

A Thorough Understanding of the Type of Training the Organization Needs. The STEM model provides organizational decision makers with a comprehensive analysis of what kind of training they need. The task analysis directly links the organization's strategic objectives to training because you develop a list of all the jobs that must be performed in order to support the strategic objectives and the knowledge, skills, and abilities associated with those jobs.

Inadequate Training Resources or No Sense of Where to Find Resources, Assistance, and Training Expertise. The STEM model will help an organization determine the number of training programs it needs, as well as their associated costs and necessary resources. Organizations with type "A" or "B" cultures have made a commitment to put employees first, so they already understand the importance of allocating adequate resources for training. Organizations with type "D" or "F" cultures tend to be underperformers precisely *because* they are not concerned with developing the skills and abilities of their people.

Lack of Management Commitment to Training. From a practical perspective, management's commitment to training hinges on whether or not leaders believe that the training will produce or improve products and/or services. Training significantly adds to the output value of a product or service when it's directly linked with the strategic objectives set by management. If training is linked to organizational strategy, it encourages managers to support the training, because they know it will have a major impact on organizational competitiveness and success. Another variable that influences management's support for training is the degree to which the training has been proven or measured to enhance employee productivity and performance.

Strategic Training: Putting Employees First

Management Commitment to Training

| Management's support for training (*M*) | = | Linking training with the strategic objectives set by Management (*a*) | + | Degree to which training has been proven or measured to enhance employee productivity and performance (*b*) |

$a + b = 1$ (in percentage terms, 100%)

Where:

a has a scale going from .5 down to 0:

    .5 = fully linked with strategic objectives
    0 = no link to strategic objectives

Organizations with:

    Type A cultures = .5
    Type B cultures = .4
    Type D cultures = .3
    Type F cultures = .2 to 0

b has a scale going from .5 down to 0:

    .5 = effectiveness of training is highly documented
    0 = no measurement of the effectiveness

Organizations with:

    Type A cultures = .5
    Type B cultures = .4
    Type D cultures = .3
    Type F cultures = .2 to 0

This equation must be modified by the degree to which management accepts the organizational principle of putting employees first. Organizations that put this principle into practice tend to be more receptive to requests to allocate organizational resources for training.

Management's Commitment to Training:

$$M = \frac{a + b}{c}$$

Where c is the degree to which organizations adopt the principle of putting employees first. Organizations with:

Type A cultures = 1   Type D cultures = .8
Type B cultures = .9   Type F cultures = .7

Organizations with Type "A" cultures would have a management commitment to training score of:

$$M = \frac{.5 + .5}{1} = 1 \text{ or } 100\%$$

Organizations with Type "B" cultures would have a management commitment to training score of:

$$M = \frac{.4 + .4}{.9} = .88 \text{ or } 88\%$$

Organizations with Type "D" cultures would have a management commitment to training score of:

$$M = \frac{.3 + .3}{.8} = .75 \text{ or } 75\%$$

Organizations with Type "F" cultures would have a management commitment to training score of:

$$M = \frac{.2 + .2}{.7} = .57 \text{ or } 57\%$$

to

$$M = \frac{0 + 0}{.7} = 0 \text{ or } 0\%$$

Organizational competitiveness and success are each linked to management's commitment to training. It is this linkage that will convince management to support training.

Appropriate Skill Sets. Skill sets refer to the collective abilities of the labor pool within a community. This kind of geographical workforce need should be evaluated during the strategic planning process when locality decisions are being considered. A task analysis can further refine what kind of training will be required to accomplish the strategic objectives. After a task analysis is done, the organization should identify the employee target market and develop specific training programs for that group of employees.

A Positive Environment Where Employees Want to Excel and Are Motivated to Learn and Develop Their Skills and Abilities. As we said in Chapter 2, positive and productive work environments at the group level (and preferably organization-wide) are shaped and sustained or not sustained by each member of the organization, at each level. Most learning theories emphasize the importance of having a work environment where each employee knows that he or she is respected and valued and where employees are encouraged and allowed to be part of the decision-making process governing their work areas.

How can an organization predict how well an employee will perform on the job? The best predictor is job fit: matching the intellectual and physical abilities of an employee to the job. When there is a mismatch—when the abilities of the employee are not the abilities needed to get the job done well—you have a marginally performing employee. Marginally performing employees are unmotivated underachievers who limit organizational competitiveness and success. However, when there is a good fit between employee ability and the job, the stage is set for high productivity and product output value.

Organizations that understand and respect their employees' capabilities can motivate their employees and develop their potential, which ultimately benefits the organization. All this begins with the commitment to put employees first, which means, among other things, developing quality training programs.

How the STEM Model Can Help Organizations

Group and Organizational Success

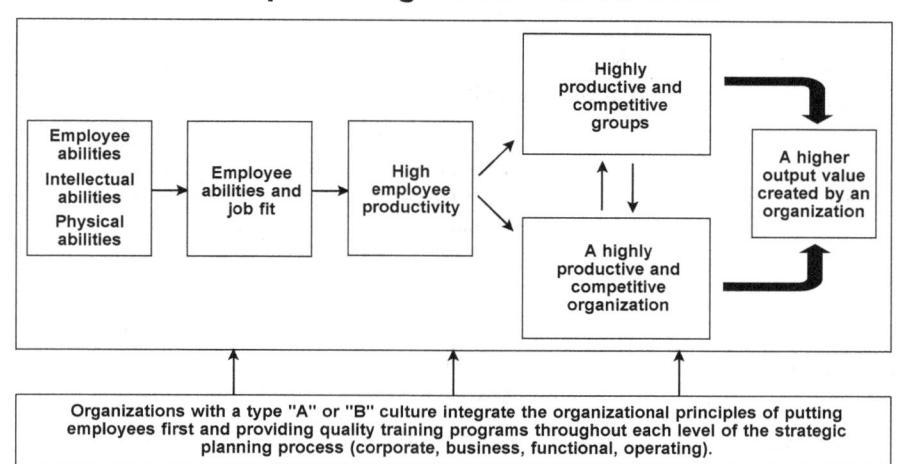

```
Employee abilities
Intellectual abilities
Physical abilities
    →
Employee abilities and job fit
    →
High employee productivity
    →
Highly productive and competitive groups
    ↕
A highly productive and competitive organization
    →
A higher output value created by an organization
```

Organizations with a type "A" or "B" culture integrate the organizational principles of putting employees first and providing quality training programs throughout each level of the strategic planning process (corporate, business, functional, operating).

Using the STEM Model to Develop a Specific Training Program

We've demonstrated how training needs can be addressed by applying the STEM model. Let's conclude this chapter by illustrating how the STEM model can be used to create a specific training program.

STEM Application Example #1

Analysis at the Macro-Organizational Training Level	
Training situation	A major U.S. bank has decided to expand its consumer credit operations. As a result of this strategic decision, a task analysis was conducted. It was determined that 40 new credit analysts in four regional offices would require training.
Analysis at the Micro-Organizational Training Level	
Employee target market	The director of training will work closely with each of the regional offices and HR to identify the employees who will be trained.

(continued)

STEM Application Example #1 (concluded)

Product content objectives	Lecture combined with credit analysis problem sets. E-training (distance learning) will be utilized to eliminate travel and lodging costs.
	The trainer assigned to develop this training program will meet with the senior consumer credit analyst (who will be a co-presenter, with the trainer) to determine what will be presented during the training session.
Place objectives	Off-the-job training in a classroom setting located in each of the four regional offices. Equipment and supply costs are illustrated in the cost analysis.
Promotion objectives	Since the director of training is a member of the strategic planning committee, the development of the training program can begin immediately.
	The credit analyst training will be highlighted in the bank's newsletter.
Price objectives	Because of the strategic significance of consumer credit analyst positions, management has decided that an in-house training program should be developed. Therefore, no cost analysis needs to be conducted regarding the purchasing of a training program from a consulting firm.
	Total cost of the training: $30,093.76 (see the cost analysis sheet)
Implementation, feedback, and evaluation	A comprehensive test will be given at the end of the training. Any trainee whose score is less than 90 will be required to take the test again after three days of additional study preparation. Communication between the trainer and the trainee during this period of time will be via e-mail.
	Two weeks after the training, the director of training will meet with each credit office manager to review the performance of the new credit analysts. Reviews will be conducted using distance learning hookup to eliminate travel and lodging costs.

Cost Analysis Sheet for Example #1

Training Costs

DIRECT MATERIAL COSTS

Direct material costs are the costs of the materials directly used in developing and running a training program.

Training Item and Explanation	Total Cost
Instructional package consisting of forms and training materials ($20 for each of the 40 trainees, plus packets for trainer and senior credit analyst). Total packets: 42	$ 840.00
Miscellaneous supplies ($2 for each of 40 trainees, plus trainer and senior credit analyst)	84.00
TOTAL DIRECT MATERIAL COSTS	$ 924.00

DIRECT LABOR

The cost of direct labor: salaries, wages, and fringe benefits directly involved in developing a training program.

Training Item and Explanation	Total Cost
Trainer Costs (salary and fringe benefits):	
Trainer salary: $30,000 (40 hours/week x 52 weeks/year = 2,080 annual hours, which equates to $14.42/hour)	N/A
Fringe benefits (35% of salary = $10,500 for 2,080 annual hours, which equates to $5.04/hour)	N/A
Time spent with senior credit analyst preparing training program (2 days x 8 hours/day @ $14.42/hour)	$ 230.72
Time spent in training class (3 days x 8 hours @ $14.42/hour)	346.08
Post-training for trainees who fail the comprehensive test (3 days x 4 hours/day @ $14.42)	173.04
Fringe benefits (52 total hours @ $5.04/hour)	262.08
Total Trainer Costs	$ 1,011.92

(continued)

Strategic Training: Putting Employees First

Cost Analysis Sheet for Example #1 (continued)

Other Training Department Costs (salary and fringe benefits):	
Director of Training salary: $95,000 (2,080 annual hours, which equates to $45.67/hour)	N/A
Fringe benefits (35% of salary = $33,250 for 2,080 annual hours, which equates to $15.98/hour)	N/A
Meetings with credit managers: 4.5 hours + 2 hours with trainer (6.5 hours @ $45.67/hour)	$ 296.85
Fringe benefits (6.5 hours @ $15.98/hour)	103.87
Clerical support (8 hours @ $6.50/hour)	52.00
Clerical fringe benefits (8 hours @ $2.28/hour)	18.24
Total Other Training Department Costs:	**$ 470.96**
General Organizational Support (salary and fringe benefits):	
Senior Credit Analyst salary: $35,000 (2,080 annual hours, which equates to $16.82/hour)	N/A
Fringe benefits (35% of salary = $12,250 for 2,080 annual hours, which equates to $5.89/hour)	N/A
Time spent (2 training preparation days + 3 training days x 8 hours/day @ $16.82/hour)	$ 672.80
Fringe benefits (2 training preparation days + 3 training days for 8 hours/day @ $5.89/hour)	235.60
Credit office manager's average salary: $99,000 (2,080 annual hours, which equates to $47.59/hour)	N/A
Fringe benefits (35% of salary = $34,650 for 2,080 annual hours, which equates to $16.66/hour)	N/A
Total cost associated with credit managers (4.5 hours x 4 credit managers @ $47.59/hour)	$ 856.62
Fringe benefits (4.5 hours x 4 credit managers @ $16.66/hour)	299.88
Total General Organizational Support	**$ 2,064.90**
TOTAL DIRECT LABOR COSTS	**$ 3,547.78**

How the STEM Model Can Help Organizations

Cost Analysis Sheet for Example #1 (continued)

OVERHEAD COSTS	
Overhead costs for training: all other training costs associated with the development of a training program, other than direct materials or direct labor.	
Training Item and Explanation	**Total Cost**
Trainee Costs (salary and fringe benefits):	
Trainee salary: $22,000 (2,080 annual hours, which equates to $10.58/hour)	N/A
Fringe benefits (35% of salary = $7,700 for 2,080 annual hours, which equates to $3.70/hour)	N/A
Time spent in training class (3 days x 8 hours/day @ $10.58/hour for each of 40 trainees)	$ 10,156.80
Post-training for trainees who fail comprehensive test (3 days x 4 hours @ $10.58 for 4 trainees. Assume that 4 of the 40 trainees will fail comprehensive test.)	507.84
Fringe benefits (24 training hours @ $3.70/hour for each of 40 trainees, plus 12 post-training hours @ $3.70/hour for each of 4 trainees, which equates to $3,552 + $177.60)	3,729.60
Total Trainee Costs	**$ 14,394.24**
Loss of Productivity while Training	
Daily work not being performed while trainees are attending the training session (24 training hours @ $6.50/hour x 40 trainees + 12 post-training hours @ $6.50/hour x 4 trainees, which equates to $6,240 + $312)	$ 6,552.00
Fringe benefits (36 hours @ $2.28 x 40 trainees, plus 12 hours @ $2.28 x 4 trainees, which equates to $2,188.80 + $109.44)	2,298.24
Total Loss of Productivity (while training)	**$ 8,850.24**

(continued)

Cost Analysis Sheet for Example #1 (concluded)

Equipment and Hardware:	
Distance learning network: hookup and equipment fee for each of 3 days of training x 8 hours/day @ $55/hour	$ 1,320.00
Director of Training meeting with credit managers ($55/hour x 4.5 hours)	247.50
Total Equipment and Hardware Costs	**$ 1,567.50**
Refreshments (3 training days @ $5/day for each of 40 trainees, plus trainer and senior credit analyst)	$ 630.00
Facilities expense ($15 room cost/day x 3 days at each of 4 regional offices)	$ 180.00
Travel and lodging	$ 0.00
Supplies	$ 0.00
Total Overhead Costs	**$ 25,621.98**
Total Cost for Training Program	**$ 30,093.76**
Cost/Trainee ($30,093.76 for a total of 40 trainees)	**$ 752.34**

STEM Application Example #2

Analysis at the Macro-Organizational Training Level	
Training situation	The vice president of general merchandise for a grocery retailer (i.e., Kroger or Wegmans) has decided to develop a merchandise-display training program to set consistent merchandising display standards. The training program will initially involve 10 stores located in Massachusetts. As a result of this strategic decision, a task analysis was conducted. It was determined that general merchandise department managers would require training.
Analysis at the Micro-Organizational Training Level	
Employee target market	The general-merchandise department managers at the 10 stores in Massachusetts.
Product content objectives	Demonstration and practice sessions. The trainer assigned to develop this training program will meet with the vice president of general merchandise to determine the specific merchandise techniques and company display standards. A video of the training session will be made for future training purposes.
Place objectives	The training will be conducted at the most centrally located store in order to reduce travel expenses. Equipment and supply costs are illustrated in the cost analysis.
Promotion objectives	Since the director of training is a member of the strategic planning committee, the development of the training program can begin immediately. The general-merchandise department managers will be notified of the training by their store manager. The training session will be highlighted in the company newsletter. The importance of establishing consistent merchandising displays will also be summarized in the company newsletter. Contests will be established and prizes awarded for the displays that best meet company standards.

(continued)

STEM Application Example #2 (concluded)

Price objectives	To minimize costs, an in-house training program will be developed. However, a local video production company has been hired to film and produce a video that will be utilized for future training. The same company will also produce an information booklet that will illustrate the merchandise displays.
	Total cost of the training: $14,822.27 (see the cost analysis sheet)
Implementation, feedback, and evaluation	An information booklet highlighting the merchandise techniques and company display standards will be distributed to the trainees. Each trainee will be expected to demonstrate the merchandise techniques by setting up an actual merchandise display that meets company standards.
	Three weeks after the training, the director of training will meet with each store manager to review the performance of the general-merchandise managers. The vice president of general merchandise will visit the stores to review the store displays and meet with store managers.

Cost Analysis Sheet for Example #2

Training Costs		
DIRECT MATERIAL COSTS		
The cost of the materials directly used in developing and running a training program.		
Training Item and Explanation		**Total Cost**
Instruction booklet ($30 for each of the trainees, plus a booklet for the trainer and vice president of general merchandising) Total booklets: 12		$ 360.00
Miscellaneous supplies ($35 for each of 10 trainees, plus trainer)		385.00
TOTAL DIRECT MATERIAL COSTS		$ 745.00
DIRECT LABOR		
The cost of direct labor: salaries, wages, and fringe benefits directly involved in developing a training program.		
Training Item and Explanation		**Total Cost**
Trainer Costs (salary and fringe benefits):		
Trainer salary: $20,000 (40 hours/week x 52 weeks/year = 2,080 annual hours, which equates to $9.62/hour)		N/A
Fringe benefits (35% of salary = $7,000 for 2,080 annual hours, which equates to $3.37/hour)		N/A
Time spent with V.P. of general merchandising preparing training program (1.5 days x 8 hours/day @ $9.62/hour)		$ 115.44
Time spent in training class (2 days x 8 hours/day @ $9.62/hour)		153.92
Fringe benefits (28 total hours @ $3.37/hour)		94.36
Total Trainer Costs		$ 363.72

(continued)

Strategic Training: Putting Employees First

Cost Analysis Sheet for Example #2 (continued)

Other Training Department Costs (salary and fringe benefits):		
Director of Training salary: $45,000 (2,080 annual hours, which equates to $21.63/hour)		N/A
Fringe benefits (35% of salary = $15,750 for 2,080 annual hours, which equates to $7.57/hour)		N/A
Meetings with V.P. of general merchandising: 1.5 hours + 1 hour with trainer (2.5 hours @ $21.63/hour)	$	54.07
Fringe benefits (2.5 hours @ $7.57/hour)		18.93
Clerical support (2 hours @ $6.50/hour)		13.00
Clerical fringe benefits (2 hours @ $2.28/hour)		4.56
Total Other Training Department Costs	$	90.56
General Organizational Support (salary and fringe benefits):		
V.P. of general merchandising salary: $75,000 (2,080 annual hours, which equates to $36.05/hour)		N/A
Fringe benefits (35% of salary = $26,250 for 2,080 annual hours, which equates to $12.62/hour)		N/A
Time spent (3 training preparation hours + 15 post-training hours @ $36.05/hour)	$	648.90
Fringe benefits (3 training preparation hours + 15 post-training hours @ $12.62/hour)		227.16
Store manager's average salary: $70,000 (2,080 annual hours, which equates to $33.65/hour)		N/A
Fringe benefits (35% of salary = $24,500 for 2,080 annual hours, which equates to $11.78/hour)		N/A
Total cost associated with store managers (15 hours for all 10 store managers, or 1.5 hours per store manager @ $33.65 and $11.78, which equates to $504.75 + $176.70)	$	681.45
Total General Organizational Support	$	1,557.51

(continued)

Cost Analysis Sheet for Example #2 (continued)

External Consulting Expense:		
Training video (15 copies of the video @ $75)	$	1,125.00
Consulting fee for producing video and information books		2,000.00
Total Consulting Expense	$	**3,125.00**
TOTAL DIRECT LABOR COSTS	$	**5,136.79**

OVERHEAD COSTS	
Overhead costs for training: All other training costs associated with the development of a training program, other than direct materials or direct labor.	

Training Item and Explanation	Total Cost
Trainee Costs (salary and fringe benefits):	
Trainee salary: $32,000 (2,080 annual hours, which equates to $15.38/hour)	N/A
Fringe benefits (35% of salary = $11,200 for 2,080 annual hours, which equates to $5.38/hour)	N/A
Time spent in training class (2 days for 8 hours @ $15.38/hour for each of 10 trainees)	$ 2,460.80
Fringe benefits (16 training hours @ $5.38/hour for each of 10 trainees)	860.80
Total Trainee Costs	**$ 3,321.60**
Loss of Productivity while Training	
General merchandise assistant managers worked 2 overtime hours (2 hours x 10 trainees x $14.72/hour overtime rate)	$ 294.40
Fringe benefits (2 hours @ $5.15/hour x 10 trainees)	103.00
Total Loss of Productivity (while training)	**$ 397.40**

(continued)

Strategic Training: Putting Employees First

Cost Analysis Sheet for Example #2 (concluded)

Equipment and Hardware		
Equipment and hardware	$	0
Refreshments (2 training days @ $5.50/day for each of 10 trainees, plus trainer)	$	121.00
Facilities expense	$	0.00
Travel and Lodging		
Average travel time (1 hour for each of 9 trainees @ $15.38 and $5.38, which equates to $128.42 and $48.41 = $186.84 x 2 return trips)	$	373.68
Gasoline cost (average travel miles: 40 for each of 9 trainees @ $3.25)		1,170.00
Average travel time for V.P. of general merchandising (3 hours/day for 3 days @ $36.05 and $12.62, which equates to $324.45 and $113.58)		438.03
Gasoline cost (total miles: 135 @ $3.25)		438.75
Lodging expense for V.P. of general merchandising (2 nights @ $90/night)		180.00
Total Travel and Lodging Expense	$	2,600.48
Merchandise display contents	$	2,500.00
Total Overhead Costs	$	8,940.48
Total Cost for Training Program	$	14,822.27
Cost/Trainee ($14,822.27 for each of 10 trainees)	$	1,482.23

Note: Future training costs for this program are expected to be reduced because of the training video. Most of the traveling costs will be eliminated, as well as the consulting fee. Travel costs are expected to be reduced by $2,100; external consulting costs will be reduced by $2,000. Projected training costs are forecasted to be $10,722.27/10 employees (or $1,072.72/employee). This represents a 27.6% decrease per employee from the original cost of training.

Critical Points in Chapter 12

Critical Point 1

A thorough hiring process and a quality training environment are critical to organizational success.

Critical Point 2

The STEM model provides an effective and efficient methodology for addressing the major training needs facing today's organizations.

Critical Point 3

Management's commitment to training can be measured by the following equation:

$$M = \frac{a + b}{c}$$

Where:
- *a* measures the link between strategic planning and training
- *b* measures the degree to which the training has proven to enhance employee productivity and performance
- *c* measures the degree to which an organization adopts the principle of putting employees first

Critical Point 4

A higher product or service output value is created when an organization commits to putting employees first and providing quality training programs.

Every book seems to set its own length. Sketching or condensing it might dilute the message.

— Dean Koontz

Productivity and the economic rewards that go with it are achieved through the people of an organization.

— Tom Peters and Robert Waterman, Jr.

Chapter 13
Organizational Survival

Despite the important role that employees play regarding organizational success, many find themselves in work environments that more closely resemble the one depicted in the following dialogue from Lemony Snicket's *A Series of Unfortunate Events: The Miserable Mill.*

> "By the way," Klaus interjected. "What is the owner's name? Nobody has told us."
>
> "I don't know," Phil replied as he stroked his dusty chin. "He hasn't visited the dormitory for six years or so. Does anybody remember the owner's name?"
>
> "I think it's 'Mister' something!" one of the men joked.
>
> "You mean you never talk to him?" Violet asked.
>
> "Talk to him? We never even *see* him!" Phil replied. "The owner lives in a house across from the storage shed, and only comes to the lumber mill for special occasions. We see the foreman all the time, but never the owner."
>
> "Is he nice, Phil?"
>
> "He's awful!" one of the other workers chimed in. The others put their two cents in as well.
>
> "He's terrible!"
>
> "He's disgusting!"
>
> "He's revolting!"
>
> "He's the worst foreman the world has ever seen!"
>
> "He is pretty bad, Phil. The guy we used to have, Foreman Firstein, was okay. But last week, he stopped showing up. It was odd. The man who replaced him, Foreman Flacutono, is very mean. You'll stay on his good side, if you know what's good for you."

What does this brief passage tell us about the culture of this organization? A disconnected and adversarial relationship between management and the employees almost always leads to underperformance, and eventually, organizational failure.

Strategic Training: Putting Employees First

We began our journey by examining the culture of an organization and explaining why the quality of the employees, at all levels, is the driving force behind productivity, competitiveness, and success in the marketplace. The employees in the most successful organizations *are* the organization, and nothing in these cultures is considered more important than developing those individuals. It's the employees who breathe life into an organization: They establish every policy and process, and they build every product and deliver the service. It's the skills and abilities of the employees that give an organization its competitiveness. Without them, there is no organization! The fundamental rule of organizational survival is to put employees first and develop their abilities and skills by establishing a quality training environment.

Group and Organizational Success

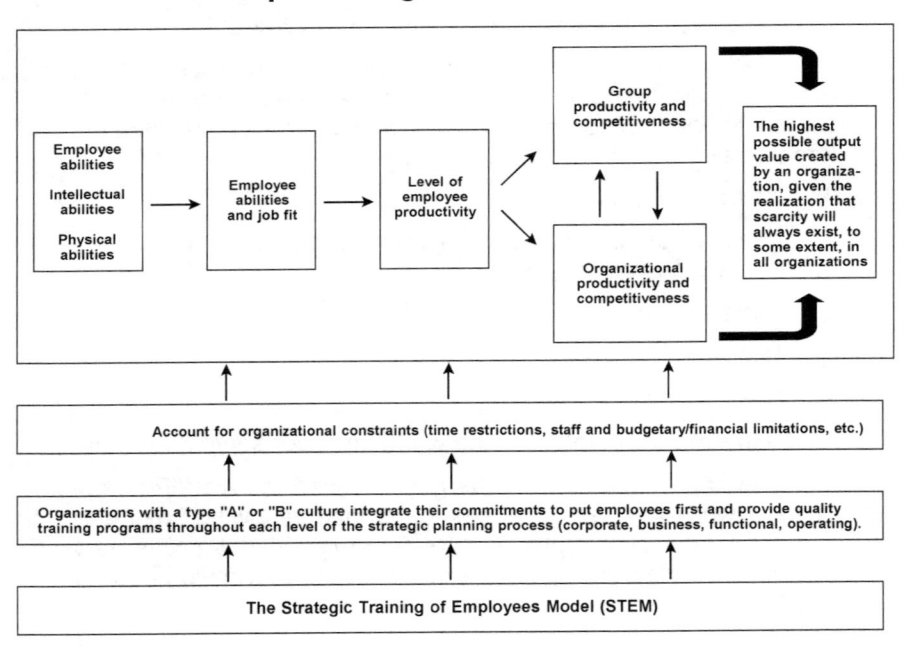

```
Employee abilities          Employee              Level of            Group productivity and         The highest possible output
Intellectual abilities  →   abilities     →       employee            competitiveness                value created by an organiza-
Physical abilities          and job fit           productivity                                       tion, given the realization that
                                                                      Organizational                 scarcity will always exist, to
                                                                      productivity and               some extent, in all organizations
                                                                      competitiveness
```

Account for organizational constraints (time restrictions, staff and budgetary/financial limitations, etc.)

Organizations with a type "A" or "B" culture integrate their commitments to put employees first and provide quality training programs throughout each level of the strategic planning process (corporate, business, functional, operating).

The Strategic Training of Employees Model (STEM)

Throughout this book, we have stressed the fact that training plays a critical role in developing the skills and abilities of a workforce, and that every organization faces time when regardless of size, resources are scarce. Scarce resources force the organization to make decisions about where resources will be allocated and the amount of training that an organization can provide (if it values training at all). The Strategic Training of Employees Model described in this book offers a way to effectively and efficiently design training and career-development programs by linking all training with the organization's strategic objectives, while still accounting for organizational constraints. An organization can use the model to generate the highest possible output value, given the realization that resources will always be scarce to some extent in all organizations.

The STEM model is based on two principles:

1. Organizations should put employees first.
2. Organizations must develop quality training programs, even though there are organizational constraints.

Practical Considerations

- All training programs must be based on the strategic objectives of an organization. The STEM model provides a practical managerial structure for developing a quality training environment.

- The framework can help you analyze for training situations and requirements, but it is flexible enough to be applied to any of a wide range of solutions, given the circumstances associated with an organization.

- The STEM model balances the need for production and the need for training.

- In the STEM model, the director of training is a key part of the strategic planning process.

- The model uses task analysis to help organizations determine what type of training they need. The task analysis is directly linked with the strategic objectives of the organization, which will help identify realistic training needs.

- Using the STEM model will increase management's commitment to training because it links training with the organization's overall strategy and emphasizes the need to collect data to measure the effectiveness of the training.

Strategic Training: Putting Employees First

- The model provides a useful framework for employee motivation because it targets the knowledge, skills, and abilities employees will need to build on in order to achieve strategic objectives. Once employees' skills and abilities match the job, the stage is set for generating high productivity and product output value.

The Strategic Training of Employees Model (STEM)

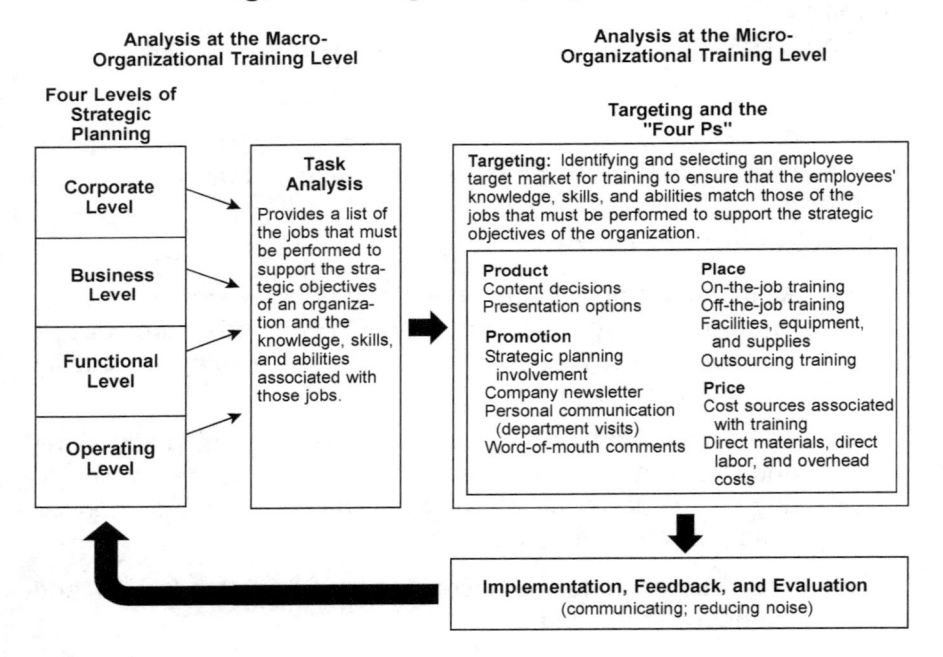

Analysis at the Macro-Organizational Training Level

Four Levels of Strategic Planning:
- Corporate Level
- Business Level
- Functional Level
- Operating Level

Task Analysis
Provides a list of the jobs that must be performed to support the strategic objectives of an organization and the knowledge, skills, and abilities associated with those jobs.

Analysis at the Micro-Organizational Training Level

Targeting and the "Four Ps"

Targeting: Identifying and selecting an employee target market for training to ensure that the employees' knowledge, skills, and abilities match those of the jobs that must be performed to support the strategic objectives of the organization.

Product
Content decisions
Presentation options

Promotion
Strategic planning involvement
Company newsletter
Personal communication (department visits)
Word-of-mouth comments

Place
On-the-job training
Off-the-job training
Facilities, equipment, and supplies
Outsourcing training

Price
Cost sources associated with training
Direct materials, direct labor, and overhead costs

Implementation, Feedback, and Evaluation
(communicating; reducing noise)

The Fundamental Rule of Organizational Survival

The quality of an organization's people, at all levels, ultimately determines the organization's success or failure. The theme of this book is putting employees first. That same subject will be explored further in subsequent works.

> Put employees first.

References

Abram, S. (March/April 2005). The Role of E-Learning in the K-12 Space. *MultiMediaand and Internet at Schools,* Vol. 12, Issue 2, p.19.

American Society for Training and Development (2004). *State of the Industry: ASTD's Annual Review of Trends in Workplace Learning and Performance.*

Bassi, L. J. (Winter 1994). Workplace Education for Hourly Workers. *Journal of Policy Analysis and Management,* Vol. 13, Number 1, pp. 55–75.

Baumol, W. J., and A. S. Blinder. (2000). *Economics: Principles and Policy.* Orlando, Florida: Harcourt College Publishers.

Becker, G. (1964). *Human Capital.* New York: Columbia University Press.

Berta, D. (September 19, 2005). Satisfaction Grows with Worker Knowledge and Confidence. *Nation's Restaurant News.* Vol. 39, Issue 38, pp. 122–126.

Biech, E. (2005). *Training for Dummies.* Hoboken, New Jersey: Wiley Publishing, Inc.

Chesteen, S., L. Caldwell, and L. Prochazka. (July 1998). Taking Legal Risks Out of Adventure Training. *Training and Development Journal,* Vol. 42, Issue 7, pp. 42–47.

Deal, T. E., and A. A. Kennedy. (1982). *Corporate Cultures: The Rites and Rituals of Corporate Life.* Reading, Massachusetts: Addison-Wesley.

Decker, P. J., and B. R. Nathan. (1985). *Behavior Modeling Training.* Westport, Connecticut: Praeger Publishers.

E-learning is Still a Priority. (March 15, 2005). *Times, The United Kingdom,* Item 7EH3331140617.

English, L. (1999). An Adult Learning Approach to Preparing Mentors and Mentees. *Mentoring and Training,* Vol. 7, Issue 3, pp. 195–202.

Finch, C. R., and J. R. Crunkilton. (1989). *Curriculum Development in Vocational and Technical Education: Planning, Content, and Implementation.* Boston, Massachusetts: Allyn and Bacon.

Finkel, C. (February 1986). Pick a Place, But Not Any Place. *Training and Development Journal,* Vol. 40, Issue 2, pp. 51–53.

Finkel, C. (July 1997). Meeting Facilities That Foster Learning. *Training and Development.* Vol. 51, Issue 7, pp. 36–42.

Galbo, C. (May/June 1998). Helping Adults Learn. *Thrust for Educational Leadership.* Vol. 27, Issue 7, pp. 13–17.

Gitman, L. J., and C. McDaniel (2003). *The Best of the Future of Business.* Mason, Ohio: Thomson/South-Western.

Gomez-Mejia, L. Balkin, D. and R. Cardy (1995). *Managing Human Resources.* Englewood Cliffs, New Jersey: Prentice Hall, Inc.

Gordon, J. R. (1996). *Organizational Behavior.* Upper Saddle River, New Jersey: Prentice Hall, Inc.

Harris, M. (2000). *Human Resource Management: A Practical Approach.* Orlando, Florida: Harcourt College Publishers.

Hellriegel, D., J. W. Slocum, Jr., and R. W. Woodman (1995). *Organizational Behavior.* St. Paul, Minnesota: West Publishing Company.

Hicks, S. (May 2000). Successful Global Training. *Personnel Management: International Business Enterprises,* Vol. 54, Number 5, p. 95.

Higley, J. (September 19, 2005). Training in Spotlight as Industry Rebounds. *Hotel and Motel Management,* Vol. 220, Issue 16, pp. 3, 81.

Hill, C., and G. R. Jones. (1998). *Strategic Management: An Integrated Approach.* Boston, Massachusetts: Houghton Mifflin.

Idhammar, C. (November 1997). Retaining Valuable Skills. *Pulp and Paper,* Vol. 71, Number 11, p. 35.

Jennings, M. (2003). *Business: Its Legal, Ethical, and Global Environment.* Mason, Ohio: Thomson/South-Western, West.

References

Joyner, J. (2001). Corporate Culture Defines Success. *Computing Canada*, Vol. 27, 26.

Juechter, M., and C. Fisher. (1998). Five Conditions for High-Performance Cultures. *Training and Development,* Vol. 52, pp. 63–68.

Keegan, W. J., S. E. Moriarty, and T. R. Duncan (1995). *Marketing.* Englewood Cliffs, NJ: Prentice Hall, Inc.

Keen, P., and S. Morton (1978). *Decision Support Systems: An Organizational Perspective.* Reading, Massachusetts: Addison-Wesley, Inc.

Kent, S. (September 6, 2005). Happy Workers are the Best Workers. *Wall Street Journal,* p. A20.

Kerr, P. (1977). *Esau: A Thriller.* New York: Henry Holt and Company.

Knowles, M. (1990). *The Adult Learner.* Houston, Texas: Gulf Publishing.

Koontz, D. (2000). *Tick Tock.* New York: Bantam Books.

Kotler, P. (1997). *Marketing Management: Analysis, Planning, Implementation, and Control.* Englewood Cliffs, New Jersey: Prentice Hall, Inc.

Kotler, P., and G. Armstrong (1991). *Principles of Marketing.* Englewood Cliffs, New Jersey: Prentice Hall, Inc.

Lamb, C., J. Hair, and C. McDaniel (2000). *Marketing.* Cincinnati, Ohio: South-Western College Publishing.

Langan-Fox, J., and P. Tan (1997). Images of a Culture in Transition: Personal Constructs of Organizational Stability and Change. *Journal of Occupational and Organizational Psychology,* Vol. 70, pp. 273–295.

Levering, R. (1988). *A Great Place to Work: What Makes Some Employers So Good (and Most So Bad).* New York: Avon Books.

Loewenstein, M. A., and J. R. Spletzer (Fall 1999). *General and Specific Training: Evidence and Implications. Journal of Human Resources*, Vol. 34, Number 4, pp. 710–734.

Maher, K. (May 3, 2005). Skills Shortages Gives Training Programs New Life. *Wall Street Journal*, p. A2.

Mankiw, G. (2004). *Principles of Economics.* Mason, Ohio: Thomson South-Western.

McCarthy, E. J. (1994). *Basic Marketing: A Managerial Approach.* Boston, Massachusetts: Irwin.

McEachern, William, J. (2000). *Economics: A Contemporary Introduction.* Cincinnati, Ohio: South-Western College Publishing.

Merrick, A., and D. K. Berman (November 18, 2004). Kmart to Buy Sears for $11.5 billion. *Wall Street Journal,* p. A1.

Mescon, M. H., B. L. Courtland, and J. V. Thill (2002). *Business Today.* Upper Saddle River, New Jersey: Prentice Hall, Inc.

Micari, M. (Autumn 2004). From Science to Citizenship: An Analysis of Twentieth-Century Trends in Corporate Rhetoric on Employee Education. *Studies in the Education of Adults,* Vol. 36, Number 2, pp. 206–221.

Millett, L. (1996). *Sherlock Holmes and the Red Demon.* New York: Viking.

Mintzberg, H. (1973). *The Nature of Managerial Work.* New York: Harper and Row.

Mission Statement Myopia. *Training.* Vol 41, Number 12, p. 16.

Moorhead, G., and R. Griffin (1995). *Organizational Behavior: Managing People and Organization.* Boston, Massachusetts: Houghton Mifflin Company.

Morgan, C. (1998). Culture Change/Culture Shock. *Management Review*, Vol. 87, Issue 10, p.13.

Morgan, G. (1997). *Images of Organization.* Thousand Oaks, California: Sage Publications, Inc.

References

Morley, P. (2001). *Coming Back to God.* Grand Rapids, Michigan: Zondervan Publishing House.

Murray, A. (May 6, 2003). Corporate Reforms Tamed Only Part of 3-Headed Beast. *Wall Street Journal,* p. A4.

Ng, A. (2001). Adventure Learning: Influence of Collectivism on Team and Organizational Attitudinal Changes. *Journal of Management Development*, Vol. 20, Issue 5, pp. 424–441.

Noe, R. A. (1999). *Employee Training and Development.* Boston, Massachusetts: Irwin/McGraw-Hill.

O'Brien, J. A. (2002). *Management Information Systems: Managing Information Technology in the E-Business Enterprise.* New York: McGraw-Hill Irwin.

Ouchi, W. G. (1981). *Theory Z: How American Business Can Meet the Japanese Challenge.* Reading, Massachusetts: Addison-Wesley.

Peters, T., and R. Waterman, Jr. (2004, 1982). *In Search of Excellence.* New York: Harper Business Essentials.

Porter, M. (1980). *Competitive Strategy: Techniques for Analyzing Industries and Competitors.* New York: The Free Press.

Porter, M. (1985). *Competitive Advantage: Creating and Sustaining Superior Performance.* New York: The Free Press.

Reich, R. (1983). *The Next American Frontier.* New York: Penguin Books.

Reich, R. B. (2002). *I'll Be Short: Essentials for a Decent Working Society.* Boston, Massachusetts: Beacon Press.

Reid, R., and N. R. Sanders (2002). *Operations Management.* New York: John Wiley and Sons.

Reigle, R. F. (2001). Measuring Organic and Mechanistic Cultures. *Engineering Management Journal.*

Renckly, R. G. (2004). *Human Resources: Barron's Business Library.* Hauppauge, New York: Barron's Educational Series, Inc.

Robbins, S. P. (1993). *Organizational Behavior.* Upper Saddle River, New Jersey: Prentice Hall, Inc.

Robbins, S. P. (2001). *Organizational Behavior.* Upper Saddle River, New Jersey: Prentice Hall, Inc.

Robbins, S. P., and D. A. DeCenzo (1998). *Fundamentals of Management: Essential Concepts and Applications.* Upper Saddle River, New Jersey: Prentice Hall, Inc.

Rothwell, W. J., and H. C. Kazanas (October 1990). Planned OJT Is Productive OJT. *Training and Development Journal,* pp. 53–55.

Sage, A. (September 1981). Behavioral and Organizational Considerations in the Design of Information Systems and Processes for Planning and Decision Support. *IEEE Transactions on Systems, Man, and Cybernetics,* Vol. SMC-11, Number 9, pp. 640–678.

Schein, E. (Summer 1983). The Role of the Founder in Creating Organizational Culture. *Organizational Dynamics,* p. 14.

Selznick, P. (February 1948). Foundations of the Theory of Organizations. *American Sociological Review.* Vol. 13, Number 1, pp. 25–35.

Simon, H. (1960). *The New Science of Management Decision.* New York: Harper and Row.

Snicket, L. (2000). *A Series of Unfortunate Events: The Miserable Mill.* New York: HarperCollins Publishers, Inc.

Thomas, D. (1988). *The Secret Cases of Sherlock Holmes.* New York: Carroll and Graf Publishing, Inc.

Thompson, A., and A. J. Stickland III (2003). *Strategic Management: Concepts and Cases.* New York: McGraw-Hill Irwin.

Training and More Corporate Involvement are HR's Top Issues for 2001: Special Report on Strategic Planning. (January 2001). *HR Focus,* Vol. 78, Issue 1.

Warren, C. S., J. M. Reeve, and P. E. Fess (1999). *Accounting*. Cincinnati, Ohio: International Thomson Publishing.

Wentland, D. (Winter, 2003). The Strategic Training of Employees Model: Balancing Organizational Constraints and Training Content. *Advanced Management Journal,* Vol. 68, Number 1, pp. 56–63.

Zikmund, W. G., and M. d'Amico (1998). *Effective Marketing: Creating and Keeping Customers*. Cincinnati, Ohio: South-Western College Publishing.

About the Author

Daniel M. Wentland has been active in the fields of business administration and economics for more than 25 years. His administrative and supervisory experience with Fortune 500 corporation Citigroup and the banking industry led to an interest in research and teaching at the college level. In 1989, he began his academic career as adjunct faculty member at several New York colleges, teaching courses in macro and micro economics, organizational behavior, marketing, and business management.

He is a full-time faculty member and coordinator of the business administration department at Holmes Community College in Jackson, Mississippi, holding an MBA and a master of science degree in marketing, as well as undergraduate degrees in both economics and marketing. He is currently working on a Ph.D. in educational leadership from Jackson State University.

Dan presents his research work at conferences, and has written for such publications as *Advanced Management Journal; Compensation and Benefits Review;* and *Education.* He lives with his wife Kathy in Brandon, Mississippi.

CPSIA information can be obtained
at www.ICGtesting.com
Printed in the USA
BVHW040245290819
557125BV00018B/396/P